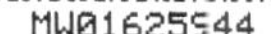

Throwing a Great Party

A Customized Edition for Broderbund Software

Phyllis Cambria and Patty Sachs

Taken from:

The Complete Idiot's Guide to Throwing a Great Party
by Phyllis Cambria and Patty Sachs

Published by Alpha Books
Indianapolis, Indiana 46290

This special edition published in cooperation with Pearson Custom Publishing.

Printed in the United States of America

10 9 8 7 6 5 4 3 2

Please visit our web site at www.pearsoncustom.com

ISBN 0-536-70660-3

BA 996161

PEARSON CUSTOM PUBLISHING
75 Arlington Street, Suite 300, Boston, MA 02116
A Pearson Education Company

Contents at a Glance

Contents

Foreword

Where was *The Complete Idiot's Guide to Throwing a Great Party* when I gave my first get-together! I could have used the expert help from authors Phyllis Cambria and Patty Sachs. Now it's all here—everything you need to know about hosting parties—in one complete reference guide.

In a simple and easy-to-follow format, party pros Cambria and Sachs invite even first-timers to host a party with "Festive Fundamentals." They offer all the basics for a guaranteed successful event, even if you're a nervous novice. The authors cover everything from awesome invitations to zippy cleanup, in a breezy, well-written style that makes this great resource fun and easy to use. They even wrap up the party information like a present, by providing sections on "Going Pro" for those who want to make party-hosting a profession.

The Complete Idiot's Guide to Throwing a Great Party is chock-full of practical party-planning tips. The sidebars are especially helpful, with lots of fast and easy ideas. Watch for quickies like "Chips and Tips" that offer general party tips and information, "Party Pitfalls" that provide warnings to watch out for, "Festive Facts" with entertaining anecdotes, and "Shindig Sayings" to help you understand popular party terms. And if you just want to cut to the chase and get to the basics for throwing a successful party, check out "The Least You Need to Know" for the nitty-gritty.

You'll find help with everything having to do with parties—planning the guest list, choosing a theme, partying without going to the poorhouse, inviting invitations, setting the stage, tasty refreshments, and helpful how-to hostess tips. The authors cover all kinds of party themes from cocktail parties to black-tie affairs, from seasonal celebrations to life's big events—for all ages and occasions. They teach us how to wind up the party gracefully when it's time for the guests to go home. And they're right there with tips on how to clean up the post-party confetti and clutter.

If that's not enough, the book contains a bonus section with Party-Planning Worksheets, offering projected budgets, party planning, and vendor guidelines. You'll find product and service resources, including reference materials, wonderful Web sites, and information on how to contact the authors. And if you need help with beverage selection, you'll find tips on how to choose and serve a variety of wines.

Finally, if you just need an excuse for a party, check out the Calendar of U.S. Holidays that offers suggestions for a full year of party options. You can celebrate Elvis Presley's birthday, Winnie the Pooh Day, National Earmuff Day, Sadie Hawkins Day, Underdog Day, and my favorite—National Dessert Day.

So what are you waiting for? You don't need an excuse to host a party, now that Cambria and Sachs are here. They've done most of the work for you, and you'll find it all in their Party Central guidebook: *The Complete Idiot's Guide to Throwing a Great Party!*

Penny Warner is the author of over 30 books, including *Kids' Pick-A-Party, Kids' Party Games and Activities, Slumber Parties, Storybook Parties, Baby Birthday Parties,* and *The Best Party Book.*

Penny Warner

Penny Warner has sold over 30 books for parents and kids, featuring ideas on parties, games, activities, snacks, and child development. Warner has appeared numerous times on San Francisco Bay Area and national television, presenting party tips for adults and children. She lives in Danville, CA, with her husband and has two grown children.

Introduction

Notes from the Authors

A note from Phyllis:

A few years ago, after almost 20 years as a professional event coordinator and part-time freelance writer, I had decided to test the book-publishing waters. However, whenever I felt I had a great idea for a book, I'd do some research and find that a certain other planner, Patty Sachs, already had the same idea and had written a book about it. If I read an article in the newspaper about party planning, Patty Sachs was often quoted. Whenever I'd talk with other coordinators around the country, Patty's name would come up in the conversation.

Finally, out of curiosity (and mild envy), I bought one of her books and learned why she was so successful. Her ideas are extremely clever and she writes books that are fun to read. Happily, her philosophy about throwing a great party matches mine, and it's the same philosophy you'll find in this book:

- Plan early.
- Themes are great.
- The party starts with the invitation.
- Follow through with all you do.
- Have as much fun planning it as you do hosting it.
- Show your guests how happy you are to have them there by choosing something special and personal to give them.
- Have a schedule of activities ready, but don't play traffic cop by insisting that guests follow it exactly.
- Serve interesting, delicious, plentiful, and appropriate food and drinks.
- Thank everyone who was a part of the event.

Over the last few years, I continued planning a wide variety of events in homes, for corporations, and for nonprofit organizations. I spoke about party planning around the country, I won numerous awards for my work, and my ideas were often featured in magazines. However, whenever someone would ask me if I had written a book, I'd say, "No, but you should check out Patty Sachs. She's written a bunch of them and I agree with everything she says."

A couple of years ago, when I first signed on to the Internet, I was astounded and delighted with all the resources that were available to me. And I felt that it was finally my turn to give something back to all the people who helped me over the years, including those anonymous millions who posted information on the Web. I decided the best way to return the favor was to answer questions for folks who needed help with something I knew about: party planning. So several times a week I'd answer party-planning questions on various message boards across the Web.

One day, a request for assistance came from another member of a party planners group trying to find a resource for a product she was seeking. The person turned out to be Patty Sachs. I was so excited! Not only was I very familiar with a manufacturer I could recommend, but I was going to be able to "meet" her and to help someone that I admired so much. I sent the information, she replied "Thank you," and that was the end of that.

Later I got a note from Patty saying, "Who are you? You have all these great ideas. Why haven't I heard of you before? Why don't you write a book?"

I wrote back and in a short time, Patty and I realized that not only did we have a lot in common and a comparable work ethic and philosophy, we also had a very similar writing style. She asked me to collaborate with her on a number of projects. The partnership has worked so well, we formed our own company, Party Plans Plus. When the proposal to write *The Complete Idiot's Guide to Throwing a Great Party* was presented to Patty, she agreed to do it, but only if I would join her, and I jumped at the chance. We are thrilled to share the knowledge that took us years to acquire, and to give you the tools to produce a party you and your friends will remember for a lifetime.

Here is what Patty has to say:

Yep, that's how it happened. I have a few more decades of producing parties than Phyllis, since I was born on my mother's birthday—and the story goes that that was the first of a lifetime of "Patty" events. The teacher in me surfaced after a few years of professional planning, when I started writing party guides, articles, and books.

The philosophy that Phyllis and I share is just that—to share. I am often asked, "Why do you give away all your trade secrets? Pretty soon no one will need your party-planning services." I just smile and say, "That's actually my goal. I'd like for everyone who wants to throw a party to have the gumption and the confidence to go right ahead and do it."

I think books like this one are the safety net that party hosts need to go out on the wire. As they say, "Knowledge is power." So the information we share with you here will give you the party power you need to produce a memorable and successful event.

From the moment the party-throwing inspiration hits you, you will be able to open this book for ground-floor party-planning guidance. From there, the steps and directions for creating everything from invitations to thank-you notes are there for you to explore, adapt, and follow. We have searched through our memory banks and file cabinets for those ideas that are tried and true. We also let our imaginations wander to bring you some of our brilliant (we modestly agree on that) brainstorms that are guaranteed to dazzle your guests.

During this project we have been e-mailing our "high fives" to each other as each chapter unfolded with our cooperative efforts. We've given you hundreds of ideas that are easy enough for the newest host to attempt, intriguing enough for the neighborhood Martha Stewart, or inventive enough for the party pro who is looking to add a couple of tricks to his or her arsenal.

Our wish for you is the success that you are striving for, whether your goal is to plan an impromptu baseball-game-watching gathering, entertain gourmet-style, produce a birthday banquet, or throw an all-out blast for your neighborhood or family reunion.

Every day holds a reason to celebrate ... so start today!

How to Use This Book

This book is carefully organized to present the tools and techniques you can use to plan the perfect party. We've broken it down into the basics so that you can see how to plan any party. We've also given you full party plans with all the details, from the invitations to the food to how to decorate, making it easy for you.

Part 1, "Festive Fundamentals," gives you all the basics of planning a party. It breaks down the party into where, who, what, where, why, and how.

Part 2, "To Party Means to Plan," might be the most important factor of throwing a successful party. To ensure that your guests will want to come back for more, you need to be careful when planning everything, from the budget to the theme to your guest list.

Part 3, "The Hostess with the Mostess ..." is key to any party. This part will show you how to be the perfect host, stock a bar, and keep everything running smoothly while you find the time to enjoy yourself.

Part 4, "Classic Occasions," is all about those times when you need to host the most basic party. Whether it's cocktails, a business dinner, or a formal black-tie gala, you'll get tips on everything from what to serve to how to serve it.

Part 5, "Seasonal Celebrations," will give you ideas on throwing a terrific holiday party any time of the year. This part doesn't just give you tips for the most popular holidays, but looks at ways to make Mother's Day, Father's Day, and even Valentine's Day special for everyone.

Part 6, "Life's Big Events," takes a look at all of life's most-important milestones and shows how you, as the host, can make them even more memorable.

Part 7, "The Party's Ooooo-ver," looks at all of those things you'll need to do to get your house back in order, get your guests off safely, and collect all those party souvenirs and photos for yourself and to share with your guests.

You'll also get a number of appendixes that include party-planning worksheets, a resource list, a wine guide, a calendar of American holidays, an anniversary gift list, and a glossary of those all-important party words.

Extras

Each chapter covers everything you will need to know in terms of planning your party. However, while writing the book we came across a number of fun facts, tidbits, and related topics that we thought might be interesting to you. These have been placed in different boxes within each chapter:

Festive Facts

When planning a party, the fun usually comes from the unexpected. For that reason we've put together many unexpected or interesting and fun facts related to the topic at hand.

Party Pitfall

Anytime you are planning a party, you are bound to run across something that will make your life harder. We've made an attempt here to warn you before disaster strikes.

Shindig Sayings

These terms and definitions are all part of the world of party planning. They will help you understand what people are talking about when you are planning your big event.

Chips and Tips

These little tips will make not just your party planning but your life outside the party easier. Be sure to read them and learn something new!

Acknowledgments

We would like to thank our editor, Jessica Faust, for putting up with two often-pooped party people and seeing our vision.

Acknowledgments for Phyllis Cambria:

I would like to thank my husband, Doug, for his patience and support; my family for their understanding while I undertook another "Phyllis project;" my parents, Pat and Jerry Mangino, for being the original party people; my "partyner," Patty Sachs, for seeking me out to join her and for all the giggles and great ideas; Bobby Rodriguez for letting me learn the event business with him; Elaine Micelli Vasquez for giving me my first writing job; my friends at the South Florida-Caribbean Chapter of the International Special Events Society for always being willing to share information; and Jeff Breslauer for his friendship, encouragement, help, and "filling in the blanks."

Acknowledgments for Patty Sachs:

There's too little space here for me to give proper and heartfelt thanks to Phyllis, my "partyner" in this project. She put her heart and soul, days and nights, and wit and wisdom into the writing of this book. She carried me through from start to finish, even though she had signed on to only "travel the road, sharin' the load." In only a dozen hours in person and hundreds of hours on the 'Net, I have gained a respect for her ethics and integrity. She's become my perfect party-planning pal! (Yeah, we talk like that.)

About writing this book, my brother and agent, Terry, said, "You should do that;" my mom, Elsie, (as always) said, "You can do that;" and my kids, Frank, Cathy, and Deena, said, "Oh no! She's doing it again!" I especially loved hearing my darling grandgirls, Jasmine, Mackenzie, Aysia, and Sophia, say, "Why's Grandma doing that?" Ah, then there's my newest grandgirly, Carly Jade, who would have said (if she could talk), "I just have to smile, and she always stops doing that." I celebrate and cherish them all.

Trademarks

Part 1

Festive Fundamentals

Throwing a party can be one of the most stressful events in life. You worry that everyone is having fun, the food tastes right, the entertainment is good enough, and even whether anyone will show up.

Relax! Planning a party should be enjoyable—even fun. In this part of the book, you'll learn the absolute basics for throwing a great party—everything from planning your guest list to choosing and hiring consultants. So whether you are planning a friend's birthday or just gathering old friends together, hold your glass high and say, "Cheers, I can do this."

Chapter 1

Home Is Where the Party Is

In This Chapter

- Making your home ready for a party
- Preparing the party food
- Reasons to throw a party
- Planning your party

There are so many different excuses you could make to not have a party: You don't know who to invite, you don't have the room, it will take too long to plan, you have nothing to celebrate, or even that you just don't know how to cook. Relax! Planning and throwing a party should be fun and exciting … and easy.

In this chapter, you'll learn that the best way to throw a party is in your own home, and sometimes the best kind of party is one that just happens. You don't have to be celebrating a milestone event, and you don't even need to have more than two people. A party is a feeling, and a special way to celebrate that feeling. So sit back and learn how to turn your small apartment or house into Party Central and to throw the party of a lifetime.

Taking the Party Home

When planning a party, one of the first great worries is where the party should be. Well, that's easy—at home, of course. You probably think you don't have enough room, right? Wrong! While most homes aren't set up for ballroom dancing or hula hoop contests, there are ways to adjust and arrange the space to be more party-ready and they're all outlined in Chapter 10, "Setting Up Your Space."

What if you want to go beyond just chips, dips, and the stereo? What if you really want to go whole hog to make a theme-party extravaganza? You probably need to rent a space for that, right? Wrong again! Whether you want to set up your dining room as a disco or turn your rec room into a recording studio, you can do it.

Given a generous lead time, the proper materials, and some help from talented hands, you can accomplish these decoration dreams with relative ease. Unlike a rented party site, where rules and limitations can cause you deadline stress, an at-home party gives you 24-hour access to your party site—meaning that these preparty setups can be almost stress-free.

Party Pitfall

Do not plan major remodeling or redecorating jobs before your home party. No other project causes as much stress while taking the fun out of your party preparation. It just adds unnecessary pressure to the party process.

Shindig Sayings

An **on-site caterer** provides food for party guests at a hotel, banquet hall, restaurant, or private club.

Home Cooking

So now that you know where the party is going to be held, the next step is to plan the rest. Neglecting the details about food, drink, and even decorations could be the biggest mistake you make, so plan well.

Serving refreshments that are appropriate to your tastes, budget, and the event is another perk of entertaining at home. Unlike most banquet centers, restaurants, or hotel catering departments, you can select a menu from your favorite cookbooks, magazines, newspapers, or Web sites. There is no limit to the types of food and beverages you can serve in your own home.

If you plan a party with an *on-site caterer,* you will need an accurate head count so they know how many guests to serve. When you plan a party at home, you need only be prepared for your best guess, according to your invitation responses.

Hiring a caterer to come into your home is much different because you can find one with specialties that match your party's needs.

If a caterer isn't for you, organize an old-fashioned potluck get-together. Ask all your guests to bring a dish to share. Just make sure you find out what people are bringing so you don't end up with a table full of chocolate chip cookies.

When none of these options appeals to you, there are always the old standbys—fill bowls full of pretzels, chips, and dips, or order take-out. Too often we get wrapped up in the food, and we forget that a party is really just an excuse for friends to gather and have fun.

Timing Is Everything

A party at home means that you are under no time constraints. No one is going to tell when to start or when the fun is over. You don't have to watch the clock and sweat per-hour site fees. You also don't have to rush your guests out to make room for the next gang of revelers.

Party Pitfall

When planning a party, be sure to look into municipal ordinances or your community or condo association rules. Are there any rules regarding noise or party times? You don't want to plan your party to begin at 8 P.M. if your association rules say there can be no parties after 9 P.M.!

Let's Get Together

The reasons for getting together are as many and varied as there are hosts with an imagination and a willingness to entertain. The simplest reason (the first time you balance your checkbook) could spur you on to planning a large bash with dozens of guests, while an extra-special occasion (a silver wedding anniversary) might inspire you to arrange only a small, intimate gathering for a few dear people.

The real secret to success is to plan your work and work your plan. Do it right, from concept to conclusion, and you can have as much fun planning the party as you have at the party.

Milestone events like birthdays, anniversaries, graduations, weddings, and retirements are generally viewed as party-giving opportunities. Those are the most natural times to concoct celebrations, and they usually involve making more complex plans and inviting larger numbers of guests. If your house or apartment can accommodate the group, it makes good sense to consider having it there.

Chips and Tips

Invite one or two friends to join you as co-hosts. It not only divides the workload, it also reduces the expense, and best of all, it turns the planning process into a party-before-the-party.

Planned in a Minute ... or a Month

Think about the best party you have ever attended. Do you know if it was planned in minutes or in months? Does it matter?

It doesn't take a lot to qualify as a party. Take good company plus some tasty food and drink, and maybe add some entertainment. Voilá! You have a party! Doesn't that sound easy?

Well, it can be a piece of cake or it can be a major production—that's your choice. Obviously, the farther ahead you start planning your event, the more elaborate you can make it. That is a bonus benefit of extra lead time.

Your decision to have a party can be made months, even years, in advance. Parties can be painstakingly planned down to the finest detail—or arranged on a whim to invite folks over for that same night!

Sometimes the rush to hold a spur-of-the-moment celebration inspires instances of ingeniousness that turn out to be incredibly successful and even unforgettable. Don't let a little thing like lack of time stop you.

Festive Facts

Recently a woman who had missed her 45th class reunion called a classmate who had attended and asked her to recap the event.

While talking, they decided it would be fun to invite a few other people and share in all the stories. They made calls to a few others who, in turn, made a few calls. Before the day was out, 15 women were set to attend a potluck luncheon just two days later.

With just a brainstorm and a few phone calls, this special gathering turned out to be sentimental, hilarious, and unforgettable.

As Long As We're Here

There is often a time when you either have a small group of people in your home, or you are out with them, and the idea to have a party at your place is born.

If you are like most people, your food supply will not be adequate for a big gang. You can ask the more creative chefs to work with what's in your pantry, you can call for takeout, send some folks to the market, or, if the friends live close by, you can send everyone home to raid their own refrigerators. Remember, while food is important, fun and fellowship come first.

Once you have your improvised party buffet and bar tables set up with whatever you decide to serve, the party will likely move into full swing. Everyone is already in a festive mood from getting the grub together.

Imagine the stories that will stem from your hodgepodge home party. Without weeks of worry and woe, you have earned the "Best Host of a Last-Minute Party" award.

Chips and Tips

Have a bunch of leftover mismatched items from a number of parties? Set them out along with a collection of decorative party props. Call it a *Sanford and Son* celebration—the original trash tycoons!

And It's Good for You

Mental health experts all agree that celebration is good for you. It makes sense. Whenever you gather with others to pay tribute to someone or to just be together, your sense of well-being gets a boost.

Holidays and milestone occasions need not be the only times your family and friends gather. You can open your home to them for reasons real or invented.

Good for a Child's Heart

Children thrive at parties when adults are there to pay special attention to them. The impromptu celebration to acknowledge an accomplishment of a child is worth 10 times the labor that goes into producing it. Auditioned for the play, but didn't get the part? He deserves a party just for trying out. Passed an exam to bring a C up to a B? This definitely calls for a party.

Festive Facts

A 13-year-old boy hated every minute that he had his braces on. Once they were finally removed, he decided to throw a huge party in honor of his "new teeth." His smile was from ear to ear as he enjoyed a menu of his "before braces" favorite foods—popcorn, caramel, and peanut butter.

So often these small but significant victories are overlooked when, with just a little effort, you can give your child the best gift of all—a lift in self-esteem. To put a smile on a child's face, there are no better words than "congratulations," "great job," or "I'm proud of you." A paper crown, a few balloons, a frozen pizza, and a plate of cookies are all you really need to make a party that will be remembered forever.

As you read on, you will learn all the tactics and strategies to simplify and enhance your home parties. You'll develop the confidence to look for new reasons to celebrate. When you are appointed, by yourself or by others, to meet a party challenge, you will share in the great rewards of hosting a houseful. You will experience the thrill of watching people you care about relax and enjoy themselves. They'll feel the stress of their lives melt in the embrace of your celebration. Those you pay tribute to will feel bathed in the warmth of your welcome. Follow your urge to wine and dine. Each time you plan an event or give folks an opportunity to celebrate life, you will not only make merry with them, but you will be one step closer to being a real party pro.

The Least You Need to Know

- Having a party at home gives you a wider selection of foods to serve.
- Utilize the yard, patio, garage, or deck to make your party space bigger.
- Get the help of your guests when a spontaneous party is planned.
- Celebrations are good for your heart and your soul.

Chapter 2

People Make the Party

In This Chapter

- Putting together your guest list
- How to add fresh faces to the usual crowd
- Planning a family gathering
- Preparing a party for your business associates

Who you invite to your party is often the most difficult part of planning the whole event. Your guest list is determined by many things, with the reason for the event or occasion being the most important. You generally include mostly family and dear friends to a birthday, anniversary, or wedding party. This list is the easiest to prepare. When you are planning an event like a graduation or retirement party, however, the scope of guests broadens to include neighbors, schoolmates, and work associates.

The decisions whether to invite this person or that can be difficult when your space and budget are limited. Everyone cannot be invited. Instead of being afraid you might commit social suicide, read on to discover a few guidelines to follow when you set your invitation list.

The Pulse of the Party

Your guests do not show up at your party just to see your home, eat your food, or drink your beverages. Although that is part of why they accept your invitation, the biggest motivation is to be with you and your other guests. This is true whether it is a

Chips and Tips

Throw a party where each regular member of the group is asked to bring someone new to freshen up the collection of faces.

Chips and Tips

Check with your caterer to find ways to save money. Big money savers often include holding the party on an off day—mid-week or a Sunday afternoon—and serving just hors d'oeuvres, or not serving alcohol.

special celebration or just a small get-together. People, their personalities, their differences, and their similarities are the magic ingredient of a wonderful party. How they interact to enjoy themselves is the real success element for your event.

In the initial planning stages of your party you will always have a set guest list in your mind—those nearest and dearest to you.

When it is possible, though, it is a good strategy to bring in a few new faces to add a different dimension to your established party cast.

Whether you are adding new faces or just inviting the same old crowd, the guests are what really make the party.

Organizing Your List

In an ideal world we would always be able to invite everyone we want to a party, and they would all get along. Unfortunately, we don't live in an ideal world, and when planning a guest list there are a number of things every party planner must consider.

You have to know how much you can afford and how many people your space holds. Probably the most difficult thing you'll have to do though, is *not* invite people.

Here are some quick and easy tips for facing those guest list challenges.

Less Means More

When you have a large guest list and your budget is small, it is a good idea to cut down on elaborate plans to be able to include more people. The budget for a five-course steak dinner for a dozen guests, for instance, may be stretched to feed chicken casserole to 25.

When throwing a party in your home, remember that being able to invite all those whom you wish to share your special day with is far more important than serving fancy foods and beverages.

Making the Cut

When making a guest list, it is imperative to know how to make cuts. It just isn't always possible to invite everyone you want. True, there are times when the list is not negotiable—everyone on it is a "must." However, those times are generally few and far between. For the most part, you are given the chance to review a list and make decisions based on how many people you can reasonably have at your party.

Unfortunately, there will also be times when the guest of honor will provide you with a guest list. For crowd control, suggest a maximum amount. Even the most gracious host must draw the line somewhere, so be realistic about your budget and home's limits.

If the roster is left up to you, begin by listing the guest of honor, immediate family, and a few of his or her closest friends. Then, if you have the option, start adding in other friends, followed by more distant relatives, and so on.

Another option to the growing guest list is an open house. An open house is when you set a time for your party and people are free to come and go as they please. One of the biggest advantages of an open house is that not all of the guests are usually there at one time, so you can often stretch the list.

If you are concerned about your open house getting out of hand, you might want to send guests invitations that stagger the party's hours. However, be sure that the same or comparable refreshments are available throughout the entire event. This will help avoid some people feeling as if they were invited to dinner, while others were invited only for dessert.

Party Pitfall

The idea, in theory, behind an open house is that guests will come and go throughout the course of the party. However, sometimes the bulk of the guests show up at the same time. Or, they are having such a good time, they don't want to leave. This can really wreak havoc on your plans to control the number of guests at your party, so don't over-invite.

There's One in Every Bunch

Do you have someone on your family list that stands out as a troublemaker, the proverbial "bad apple"? This is the person who doesn't think anything is done right. With some family feuds, you may have one guest threaten not to attend if a certain other person is invited.

Do not fall into this blackmail bin. As the host you have the right to do as you please—it is your party. Even though it might be difficult, invite whom you want.

There are ways around these social landmines. To begin with, you need to "know thy enemy"—that is, if you are prepared going into it, you can take steps to diffuse the situation before it becomes a problem.

Ask for help from the party spoiler, the one who does nothing but criticize. Tell him or her that his or her help will make the party a success.

This personal involvement will invariably distract him or her. After all, who wants to malign an event you had a hand in planning?

For the Hatfield and McCoy elements, invite both and give them the option to attend. Be honest with them. Explain that you would love to have them in attendance; however, you will not tolerate any open hostility. Ask them to make an effort to bury the hatchet—preferably not in each other's heads—and attend. Remind them how important they are to the guest of honor; stroke their egos. Then give them the option to decide.

Chips and Tips

If at all possible, separate the warring factions by distance (place them in separate rooms) or time (give them different arrival and departure times). You also might want to assign one or two other guests to chaperone the guests and act as a buffer should any interchanges occur. (A first aid kit and 911 on speed dial are probably not bad ideas, either.)

Party Pitfall

Double-check your guest list with another close friend to prevent forgetting anyone.

For the guest who is there only to eat the food and watch the game, take him out of the picture ... literally. Set up a TV in another room, as far away from the party as possible, and put the couch potato in there. Give him food and beverages and tell him he can keep the door shut so no one will disturb him.

He gets to watch the game; you lose the bump on the log and a major distraction.

As you can see, whatever the negative situation, it's possible to turn it into a positive.

Gathering the People Together

There are dozens of ways you can prepare a guest list and plan a party. You could choose to throw a bash for friends only, a family reunion of sorts, or include business associates. Whichever way you choose to go, the list will still take planning and preparation.

You Gotta Have Friends

Good friends don't need a reason to have a party. Being together while doing anything is fun, relaxing, and—for the most part—nurturing to the relationships. That is one of the most rewarding parts of friendship.

When you host a party for your close friends, you have the best of all worlds. You know all about these people. You can anticipate their likes and dislikes, indulge their foibles and fantasies, and help them achieve their goals and ambitions. With all of this inside knowledge, you can plan a party that fits this group like a gala glove.

The list is easy. Except for an occasional addition of friends of friends, it is set in "plaster of party." A gala or wacky invitation builds the event anticipation, and word of mouth will get this invitation out on the "friend network" within hours.

It's a Family Affair

Hosting a party for your family is probably the easiest of all scenarios. Forgiving and understanding all your shortcomings, emergencies, and phobias, your family members will either pitch in to help or simply accept your oversights.

You might have fallen into the family pattern of doing every party the same way. Why not be totally individual with your next one? Dare to be different. Throw off tradition now and then and surprise your kinfolk.

Send an invitation to each member of the family, one to the parents and one to each child. That special touch will get the youngsters enthused about attending another one of those "family" deals.

There are many ways to do it. Put together a theme party, surprise them with a distant relative, make it a formal dinner instead of a barbecue, or hire some entertainment. Have fun and turn your ho-hum party into a home run.

Chips and Tips

Occasionally, if room permits, allow teenaged children to bring a friend. This is the age when any time away from friends is almost torture for a kid.

Mixing Business with Pleasure

As we get older, we often make friends with the people we work with. We find ourselves socializing with them, not only during our lunch hour, but also in the evenings and on weekends.

These friendships are sometimes different than the friends we made through other routes. When fellow employees take time to enjoy each other outside the workspace, it is often relaxing and helps to raise morale. These get-togethers sometimes occur even more regularly than get-togethers with friends or family.

Entertaining business friends and associates should be done thoughtfully and carefully. Remember, you don't want any of these people to remember that you stripped on the dining room table after throwing back a few too many.

Party Pitfall

Choose how you plan to entertain co-workers carefully. While these occasions may seem social, there are sometimes road hazards to be aware of. In a business relationship, your co-worker today may be your boss tomorrow. Likewise, someone who works for you might one day leapfrog past you.

Have fun, of course. But be aware. Plan this event as carefully as you might plan a business presentation.

Unless you are the boss, it is rare that a work-related party would be held at your home. If this situation does arise, ask to have a committee work with you. This will allow a number of key people to have input toward the event.

Have the first committee meeting at your home so the group can survey your surroundings and make suggestions that fit the space. As host, you will likely be in charge of the committee. This is a chance to take a leadership role and make sure each committee member shines. They, in turn, will allow you to shine as well.

Chips and Tips

When you are the low person on the totem pole and you would like to move up the ladder, this type of social event can work in your favor. If it's unlikely that you will be given extra responsibilities at the office, putting together an exceptional event will enable others to see you as more responsible or socially capable than you are currently viewed.

Kids Are Guests, Too

Whether you have children or not, there will be times when kids are in your home for a party. If you plan for your home to be party central for a group of tots or teens, there are certain preparations that must be made.

The first consideration is often food. Make different food and beverage choices for the children than you would for the adults.

Get input from the parents or try to blend popular junk food with appealing but healthy choices; that way, the parents won't panic and the kids won't balk at what is being served. Just make it a kid-friendly menu.

It is a big challenge to keep toddlers and preschoolers amused, happy, and safe. To enable you and your guests to socialize, recruit older kids to help with the youngsters by paying them to baby-sit.

If the entertainment on hand isn't suitable for your young guests, ask parents to bring a child's favorite toys or videos with them.

Remember, entertainment planned for young guests must be suited to their age and the space you have for them. There are dozens of books and Web sites that offer ideas and directions for games and activities designed to occupy kids of all ages.

Chips and Tips

Dollar stores often sell dozens of items like plastic chairs, dishes, cups, and utensils that can be personalized by painting the child's name on them to use and then take as favors.

Groups and Troops

If you or one of your family members belong to an organized group or team, there is a good chance that you will get your turn to host an event.

When it comes time to gather at your home, the plans can be easy and uncomplicated. Since these events are usually very short in duration, they often require providing little more than pizza and beer, wine, or soda. It can even be a potluck supper where all you supply are the drinks and dishes.

It is also possible that you could be called upon to entertain in a more formal way, perhaps for a recognition dinner or a going-away tribute. You, then, will often find yourself working with a committee or cohost at these events.

There are also those get-togethers that are very impromptu. For instance, an important but unexpected game victory makes a big celebration mandatory. So stock up on party goods to keep on hand and have some take-out menus handy for hosting the home team.

Party Pitfall

Depending upon their age, children have a short attention span. It is better to have a large variety of amusements that will keep them constantly entertained.

Festive Facts

The term **fan,** as in an adoring or loyal fan, is derived from the word *fanatic,* someone with the highest degree of enthusiasm for a hobby or pastime. So it makes perfect sense that if you are a fan of a sport, you are also a fanatic.

Party of Pastimes and Passions

Regularly scheduled meeting times are ideal for taking turns to entertain, especially to share an interest or intrigue. If you are a collector, crafter, or hobbyist, you most likely socialize with fellow enthusiasts to enjoy the activity that binds you together as a group.

Avid adorers of food or wine, culinary arts, flower arranging, book clubs, or home decorating hold high-tone parties at which they partake in their common delights. If you have a gathering for your in-common companions, the path is quite clear—just plan to please yourself, and you will probably please them all.

Blending Different Groups

When you pay tribute to a person, all the important people in his or her life will want to be there—friends, family, and school- and workmates. The family and friends will not always know each other, and business associates will often be unfamiliar to both. To help turn strangers into friends, print up name tags color-coded to reflect different relationships: family, friend, co-worker, classmate and so on. Be sure to include a more detailed explanation of the guest's relationship to the honored guest. For example: "JOHN SMITH, Jack's next-door neighbor" or "JANE NELSON, Jack's sister."

The Least You Need to Know

- People are the most important party element.
- It is better to downsize elaborate plans in order to accommodate many than to have an elaborate event with only a few.
- Take precautions with difficult guests *before* they become difficult.
- Stagger arrival and departure times to manage large groups at open houses.
- Make specific plans for children.

Chapter 3

Here's the Plan

In This Chapter

- Making your party planner
- Using free association to establish your theme
- Keeping a party calendar
- Putting together a file of vendors

Now that you've figured out why you're having the party, it's time to sit down and plan it from start to finish—every detail down to the toothpicks. By planning even the smallest details, you can set your occasion apart from one that later brings about an "I seem to recall that party" response.

When planning a party, your main objective is a smoothly produced event that gives your guests a feeling of comfort and welcome, and that the party was planned just for them. In this chapter you'll learn how to establish the perfect party plan.

You Could Write a Book

In the process of planning your party, you'll find it very helpful to write a book outlining every facet of your event. This will be an organized, complete record of every step taken on the way to your incredible event. It will be invaluable not only for this party, but for those you plan in the future. You will be able to look back and recognize the do's and don'ts (hopefully not too many don'ts) of throwing a smashingly successful party.

Chips and Tips

Check an office supply store for festive colored binders and index cards to help set your party mood while you plan.

To put together your party planner, you need a three-ring binder with lined paper, category dividers, clear plastic sleeves, and a zipper pocket for pencils, pens, and a calculator. You will also need a pack of 3" × 5" lined index cards to make a festivity file. Both the notebook and file will play an important part in your party plans and will be referenced throughout this chapter.

While small, impromptu gatherings will probably not need many pages—in fact, maybe just one or two—your planner and file are still invaluable resources. Even if it's just your guest list, menu, chores, contacts and shopping list, a party organizer notebook will help keep you on track.

To begin your event plan, you must first draw an overall picture of your party. Then you can begin zeroing in on tasks like making any contacts or commitments. Not until you see the vision of your entertaining endeavor can you decide what your budget and time allowance might be.

To fill in all elements of your event masterpiece, make a section for each of the following basic categories in the planner and file:

- Calendar
- The Five *W*s
- Theme
- Printed Pieces (invitations, place cards, programs, menus)
- Food and Beverage (menus, recipes, shopping list)
- Site Preparation (decorations, rentals, yard spray)
- Entertainment and Activities
- Gifts, Prizes, and Favors
- Master Budget and Shopping List

Now that you have built the categories into your planner, we'll take a close look at what should go into each category.

Let Me Count the Days

One of the first sheets in your planner will be a calendar and a timeline. List on your timeline items such as: three weeks before, mail invitations; one week before, give head count to caterer and so on. Then transfer all of that to your calendar to serve as a reminder when items are expected or needed to be done.

The Five Ws

Establishing the why, when, who, where, and what of your party is the very first step in party planning. If you've already gotten this far, you probably know why—a birthday or some other special occasion. Now it is time to determine the when, who, where, and what.

Since you know why already, it is likely that you probably have a pretty good handle on when. The day is often determined by a special occasion date, holiday, or a season. Getting more specific and selecting exact dates and times may depend on the guest of honor's and host's schedules, or on the availability of a party site. You also might want to consider the schedule of key guests whose presence is vital to the party's success.

Planning where, who, and what are variables that depend on each host.

Who's There?

So with your absolutes in mind, let's plan the ideal guest list. Depending on the event, the numbers will likely vary. All names should include their address, phone number, and e-mail address.

Where Are We Going?

Where the party is held is not just important to the party planning, but also to the guest list.

In Chapter 10, "Setting Up Your Space," you will find creative solutions to space limitations, but adjustments to your guest list might need to be made depending upon the space you have.

If you choose to rent a space, note the address, the contact, and any important details like maximum capacity and payment due dates.

> **Chips and Tips**
>
> If your at-home party can't stretch to accommodate the "must haves" on your list, perhaps you can hold the party at a friend's home or plan an open house where people will come and go.

What's That?

Now that you know why, when, who, and where, it is time to take a look at what kind of party it will be. This is usually easy to decide once you have identified who your guests are and how much space you have.

If you don't have a party theme in mind, read Chapter 6, "The Theme Says It All," to get ideas on choosing the perfect theme for your event. Once you've decided, add that to your book. Remember if there are others affected, whose feedback is important, get them involved in the process. One good way is to invite them in for a *brainstorming* party or set up a conference call or on-line chat.

Shindig Sayings

To **brainstorm** means to discuss ideas openly and spontaneously.

Congratulations! You now have all the basic elements of your party pinned down. Outline each one in the first section of your planner. This is the overall party picture.

A Theme Come True

Your next step in your planner is establishing all of your theme or scheme details. For some of the more general themes, the list of "gotta haves" is easy to make. Some are easy, while others take a little more imagination to come up with just the right ideas.

Free Association Planning

When planning your theme, make up free association lists of any persons, places, things, or events that relate to the theme in any way. At this point, don't edit your thinking. As you fine-tune your plans later, you can address feasibility and cost. Right now, just think, write, and have fun!

Once the list has been established, you can sort through it to settle on your main party aspects. Don't rule out any good, but potentially "too expensive," idea yet. Chapter 7, "Banking on a Budget," holds some budget-reining strategies for you.

Festive Facts

Margaret Mitchell, author of *Gone with the Wind,* never thought she was a very good writer and had no intention of even showing her novel to a publisher. Until one fateful day when a "friend" told her that she agreed with Margaret and that she thought Margaret was wasting her time even trying to write. This made Margaret furious and had her marching, manuscript in hand, down to a Georgia hotel where Macmillan editor Harold Latham was staying. And the rest, as they say, is history.

Party Theme: Gone with the Wind

Here is an example of a free association form for a *Gone with the Wind* party. It is unlikely that they will be able to utilize every idea, but they will be able to pick and choose to come up with a great theme party.

Food and Beverage:

Mint julep, lemonade, bourbon, branch water, fried chicken, sweet potato pie, hush puppies, black-eyed peas, collard greens, red-eye gravy, catfish, crawfish, iced tea, corn, fried green tomatoes, pralines, praline cookies, Mississippi mud pie, peanut butter cookies, watermelon, buttermilk, ham, grits, okra, shrimp gumbo, dirty rice, corn fritters, rabbit stew, pheasant, possum, quail, …

Entertainment:

Fiddle, guitar, accordion, spoons, banjo, jazz, Dixieland, Cajun-Zydeco, washboard, square dance, Virginia reel, yodelers, barbershop quartet, gospel, county fair, *Gone with the Wind*, Margaret Mitchell, Civil War re-enactments, fox hunt, steeplechase, quilting bee, …

Chips and Tips

Once your start listing items, you may need to substitute one idea for another to stay on track, so keep this list in your notebook.

Decor:

Tara, magnolias, Atlanta, jasmine, jonquils, antebellum clothes, Confederate and Union flags and uniforms, cotton, velvet drapes, Spanish moss, mansions, fireflies, hoop skirts, oil lamps, horses, foxes, …

Miscellaneous:

GWTW cast, "I don't know nothin' about birthin' babies," "As God as my witness, I'll never go hungry again," "I'll think about that tomorrow," "Frankly, my dear, I don't give a damn," …

Then pull out the components you want to focus on and break down and list estimated prices. This will help you to determine your budget.

Party-Planning-at-a-Glance Worksheet

Copy this sheet to help you record your own party ideas.

Party-Planning-at-a-Glance Worksheet

Occasion: ______________________________

Date ______________________ Time ______________________

# of Guests ______ (Are these friends, family or other?)

____

Hosts: ______________________________

Guest(s) of Honor: ______________________________

____

Special Date ______________ (actual date of anniversary, birthday, etc. if different)

Location (if other than home):

____

Theme or Motif: ______________________________

Invitation Ideas: ______________________________

____

Food Ideas: ______________________________

____

Beverage Ideas: ______________________________

____

Rental equipment needed:

____

____

Activities and game ideas:

____

____

____

Entertainment or talent needed:

____

____

Favors/gifts needed and ideas:

____

____

Photography/Videography: ______________________________

Room Decorations:
____
____
____

Table Decorations: ____________________________
____

Special Details (place cards, name tags, napkin holders):
____
____

Servers or Helpers: ____________________________
____

Special Preparations:
____
____

The Printed Word

Invitations, programs, menus, place cards, and thank-you notes play a great role in producing a complete party plan. Add maps, game instructions, song sheets, or weekend itineraries and you've come up with quite a number of items that need to be printed. Whether you choose to do it yourself or do it professionally, you need to keep track of it in your planner.

The items you store in this section (in plastic sleeves) are samples, artwork, proofs, receipts, and completed order forms for everything.

Delicious Details

If you are the chef du jour or hiring a caterer, your food and beverage pages should consist of menus, recipes, shopping lists, and costs. Notes about past parties will be helpful, so jot those down.

Plan your bar (see Chapter 9, "Tiny Bubbles: Stocking Your Bar,") and estimate drink prices. Check on what equipment you'll need to rent or buy. Also include fees for servers or bartenders.

Chips and Tips

Anytime you come home from a party, jot down what you loved and what you didn't think worked well. This will help you plan your future parties.

Potluck Pleasures

If applicable, put your potluck party assignment sheets and menu plans in the food-and-beverage section as well. Note food items promised. Give guests ideas as to what to bring that will be compatible with other dishes. This detail is extremely important to avoid duplication or missed dishes from your meal.

Festive Facts

One very clever host decided to assign potluck items according to last name initials of her guests. Unfortunately, it never crossed the host's mind that the majority of the guests, all family members, were Smiths. It was a bitter-"sweet" surprise to have each Smith show up with dessert. Assign items very carefully to avoid this.

Include all paper goods and linen costs along with food and beverage costs, rentals, and staff fees, and add to the master budget sheet.

Spruce Up the Site

Preparing your site includes everything from decorations to extra toilets. When filling out your planner, include all decoration ideas and rentals, such as extra lighting, flowers, props, and even clean-up crews.

Tally up all the costs for site preparation and add them to your master budget.

Chips and Tips

Before you start planning and shopping for your decorations, make an inventory list of everything that you already have that might be useable. Consult with your most creative thinker (second most, if you are No. 1) to come up with innovative ways to integrate them into your plan.

Send in the Clowns, the Band, the Fun

Thought we'd never get to the fun part, huh? Well, true, the enjoyment that entertainment and activities add to an event is substantial. If you don't know any performers, get referrals for reliable entertainment or talent agencies. They will be able to help you find and *book* talent. Check videotapes of likely performers and then see them in action before you hire them.

In addition to musicians and DJs, talent agencies also can help you book concessions, games, face painters, fortune-tellers, magicians, caricaturists, or other variety artists.

Collect cards from photographers and videographers whose work you like as well. Good performers, videographers and photographers usually work every weekend, so sign your contracts as soon as possible to ensure you'll get the people you want.

File all paperwork in your party planner under entertainment and activities and adjust your budget accordingly.

Shindig Sayings

To **book** talent means that you have signed a contract that they will perform at your event.

When a catalog item or an item on sale is not available when you place your order, you often will receive a **raincheck.** That means when the stock has been replenished, you will automatically be sent the item.

Something to Take Home

The best party hosts send their guests home with a memento or prize to make the party last a little bit longer. They can be trivial trinkets or total treasures. Check catalogs and search discount stores for likely items and store ideas in your planner.

Use the gifts, prizes, and favors section to save photos of your favorite finds labeled with source name, contact number and all costs. Plan to receive your items at least three weeks before your event to allow time for returns and *rainchecks*. If there is imprinting, engraving, or hand lettering, schedule your orders for delivery four weeks in advance in case reprints are needed.

Add up the cost of your gifts, prizes, and favors and post them on the master budget sheet.

Party Pitfall

The average household plumbing often will back up when used to excess, or when foreign items are thrown in a toilet. So when hosting a large outdoor party, rent a portable toilet to accommodate the overflow, so to speak, of rest room activity.

Contacts, Contracts, and Costs

Chapter 5, "When It's Time to Go Pro" goes into contract details. Just be sure to read and ask questions before you sign on the dotted line. If you feel more comfortable, have your attorney review it. Remember, without a signed contract, you have no guarantees or recourse. Keep all contracts in your planner.

Double-check with all vendors two weeks in advance of the event, and then again a few days before. Make certain you have contact numbers to reach your vendors during nonbusiness hours. Likewise, give your vendor every phone number possible to contact you should the need arise.

Chips and Tips

To avoid stress, rent or borrow a cell phone for the few days before a big event so that anyone can contact you to solve a last-minute problem.

Chips and Tips

Give a copy of the party schedule to principals such as the DJ, caterer, any entertainers, video cameraman, and photographer so that they are all on site and in sync for a flawless festive flow.

All references, estimates, bids, contracts, and worksheets should be kept in the appropriate section of your planner and fees recorded on the master budget sheet.

The Minute-by-Minute Waltz

As the party plans progress, the schedule for the event itself will come into focus. A minute-by-minute schedule will keep the party on track and assure that no detail is left unattended. Nothing will be overlooked with an air-tight schedule that regulates the flow of the party to be steady and pleasant for the guests. Party pauses can be deadly, times when nothing seems to be happening or something is happening too slowly. All of this is prevented with a "minute-by-minute waltz" dance card.

- Did you thank the guests? Yes, at 8:45, according to the schedule.
- What about handing out the favors? Sure did. At 11:00 sharp.
- I'll bet we forgot to get a photo of Grandma and Grandpa. No, between 10:00 and 11:00 all the family photos were taken.

So, be sure to set aside time during your preparations to make a printed schedule for your party.

Remember, this schedule is supposed to work for you, not against you. As long as you have hit the really important items, if your guests are having fun with sing-alongs, don't jump in and say, "Stop singing. We have to play charades now!" Play host, not traffic cop.

What's in the Cards for Us?

Remember that pack of 3" × 5" cards you were instructed to buy at the beginning of the chapter? These are your party people cards. In other words, these should contain all the pertinent contact information and any details you might need on vendors or suppliers. This way, you can slip a mini-party planner in your pocket or purse to make calls without dragging around your notebook.

The Least You Need to Know

- A party planner is invaluable to any host.
- Use a free association worksheet to help establish your party's theme.
- Include vendor's comments and dates of conversations in your party planner and contact cards.
- See performers in action before hiring them.
- Get signed itemized contracts from vendors.

Chapter 4

Party Pooling: Sharing a Celebration

In This Chapter

- Co-hosting is the simplest form of party pooling
- Create a party pool for neighbors, family, friends
- Build your own member party directory
- Raise money for your neighborhood or club
- Ease party-planning stress with a party pool

In this era of two-career families and single parenting, there is a genuine shortage of leisure time. Young families struggle to get their day-to-day money and time commitments met, and still enjoy leisure activities with each other. While we're living longer and celebrating more, we also have less time to prepare for it. This pressure could easily take all the fun out of partying.

Party pooling, even in its simplest form, can prevent that from ever happening. Truth is, the act of sharing time, goods, and talents actually allows us to benefit from and support the trend toward busy, productive family life along with the explosive celebration industry. Throwing a party can be as easy as pie—or cake—à la mode.

Won't You Join Me?

The most basic *party pooling* is co-hosting. A successful system is one where each co-host invites his or her quota of guests and shares the work and expense. Such events are often planned as social paybacks, that is where the co-hosts invite guests who have entertained them. By putting their heads, hands, and pocketbooks together, the participants of this mini-pool can produce a party where the result will not only be two or three times better for each co-host but at an investment that is one-third to one-half what would have been spent in solo-hosting.

Shindig Sayings

Co-hosting a celebration by planning to **party pool** with another friend or relative means that you share in making the guest list, doing the work, and bearing the expenses.

The first step to co-hosting is the idea meeting that takes place, preferably in the home of one of the hosts. Over brunch, lunch, or dessert (hey, it's never too soon to start the party), the team brainstorms to come up with the master plan. At this gathering, the theme, if any, is established. Often all the details, duties, and costs are discussed as well. The goal of the confab is to start turning the wheels of the party machine and building the excitement.

Throughout the pre-party planning stages, you will be following checklists and double-checking task progress to be sure no detail is overlooked. If you are the home host, you will quite likely be the "task master" or "coach." A notebook for tracking all of these assignments is a requirement; just as every good coach needs a playbook, you need your notebook.

Party Pitfall

There's always the possibility of co-hosts having small disagreements, so try to keep the planning sessions on a semi-businesslike level, while still allowing fun. If the party will take place in your home, it will probably fall upon you to referee the process and smooth over rough spots.

And what better time to rehash the party and recount the events than at the final meeting, the "party payoff" meeting. This is the time when all members submit their receipts to be tallied, the total is divided, and hosts are paid. If you have enjoyed the jokes about ladies at lunch dividing up the bill, you can imagine the scenario at this final fling.

Now It's My Turn

Another way of getting help for your party is with the "you help me and I'll help you" party pool. With this style of party pooling you form a celebration co-op club. Whenever someone in the club throws a party, the other members, or *S.W.A.P.* (Special Workers at Parties) team, chip in to help. The club doesn't need to be anything official, it is really just a few folks who like to throw parties and dislike being overwhelmed by the day-of-the-event workload.

With this reciprocal plan, the host does all the up-front organization and the S.W.A.P. team runs the gala. There generally is no exchange of money, unless a helper has made a purchase for the host. The secret to the success of this scheme is for members of the team to clear their party schedule with other team members. Two events on one night could be a party plight that could swamp the S.W.A.P. team.

Shindig Sayings

A **S.W.A.P.** team are the members of your party-pooling group who show up at your party ready to work. While they know they are there to help with any of the needed duties they are also prepared to join in the fun.

Celebration Committees

Clubs, neighborhoods, businesses, teams, schools, and church organizations are all groups who routinely throw parties the cooperative way. From the ground-floor plans to the parting word, all duties are shared in an equitable way, according to each participant's resources or available time.

Festive Facts

When a hurricane left a Florida neighborhood without electricity, residents feared their food would go bad in their freezers. Instead of letting that happen, all the neighbors got together and just cooked up everything that had thawed out and gobbled up all the frozen desserts. Without air conditioning, the neighbors enjoyed a cool evening breeze as they continued to turn a horrible situation into one that was bearable—in fact, it was fun.

Fund-raising events are a perfect example of occasions when everyone pitches in to make the function a huge success. A shared workload is an easier workload.

Diving Into the Primary Party Pool

As friends and neighbors, we join forces to drive our kids to school, team up to baby-sit for each other, and pitch in when it's painting or moving time. Like farmers who help each other to raise barns or bring in the crops, we continuously try to help others succeed.

However, when it comes to planning and throwing a party, the advantages of pooling exceed saving money and time. There is also the benefit of having additional creative abilities, enthusiasm, and energy to contribute to the party picture.

Let's say you want to throw a very special bash for your son's high school graduation. Unfortunately, once you start putting together a long guest list, start planning the many details and establishing a budget, it's likely you will be discouraged and decide to celebrate with your immediate family on a small scale instead.

Chips and Tips

For basic co-hosting, you can tap into resources found in your personal address book, but for more elaborate affairs, a full-fledged party pool will keep you from drowning in duties.

However, as a member of a party pool, you don't have to give up your dreams of paying tribute to your son's success, because you will have the resources of your party pool to keep you afloat.

With party pooling, a host can double the quality of his party without spending an extra dollar or undertaking an excessive amount of work. You will get the job done in grand style by sharing talents, equipment, labor, and resources of your party pool. Everyone wades into the winnings.

In addition to reduced stress, the benefits of being in a party pool include saving both time, in searching for party goods and suppliers, and money, for purchase or rental of items. Just think, with the money you save, you can practice the two-party system—one on Friday and one on Saturday.

Building Your Pool

Someone has to put time and energy into organizing the pool and maintaining it. If it's too much work for you, start the pool and recruit another participant to share the responsibility. As you progress in the project, more help will surface. Once the party pool is filled and ready for activity, the member rewards will come floating in.

Once built, your pool can be run in one of these ways.

1. Put together a directory of all party-pool members and their potential pool contributions (time, talent, equipment). Simply print and distribute a small directory for the members (fellow employees, relatives, neighbors, association members) to use in arranging their own pooling activities.
2. Create a system where credits are earned and spent by printing a directory and setting up a record-keeping system tracking all party-pool activity, such as what has been used by whom. This method, while a little complicated, will help eliminate any squabbles over who is always using the folding chairs and who never helps others.

Your Party Directory

Regardless of which plan you are going to follow, the next step in your party pool is producing an official directory that lists information collected from each participant. Next to each member's name, you will note his or her available contributions in goods or services. As a cross reference, items and services are listed categorically with member's name. Below is a list of the goods and services you might want to seek out.

Chips and Tips

Decorations and props created for other events are excellent pool items. A treasure chest, for instance, can be used for pirate, Renaissance, medieval, or Peter Pan parties.

Catering:

- Cooking/baking
- Barbecuing
- Bartending/serving
- Cake decorating
- Candy making

Creative arts:

- Costume design
- Crafts
- Face painting
- Floral arranging
- Sewing

Equipment:

- Catering equipment
- Tables and chairs
- Costumes
- Ice chests
- Lights
- Linens
- Plants
- Tents

Graphic and visual arts:

- Calligraphy
- Desktop publishing
- Photography/videography
- Printing
- Web site design

Professional services:

- Accounting/bookkeeping
- Cosmetology
- Fund-raising
- Legal services
- Party/event planning
- Personal services (errands, shopping, gift wrapping, baby-sitting, pet-sitting, coat check)
- Secretarial (word processing, research, filing, addressing, typing, telephones, collating, copying)

Performing arts:

- Acting/music/singing
- Dancing/choreography
- Clown
- Disc jockey
- Juggling
- Magic
- Mime
- Psychic services (handwriting, palm reading, tea-leaf reading)
- Puppetry
- Stand-up comedy

Technical support:

- Carpentry
- Construction
- Electricity
- Landscaping
- Lighting/Sound
- Plumbing
- Pyrotechnics

Transportation:

- Automobile
- Boat
- Miscellaneous (sleigh rides, snowmobiles, hay wagon, carriages, child-size train)

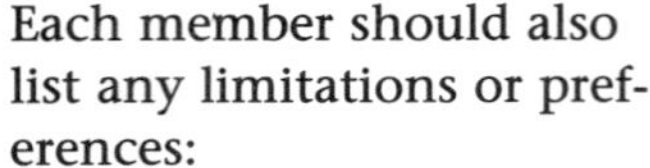

Each member should also list any limitations or preferences:

- Smoking/non-smoking
- Religious restrictions
- Available days and times
- Location restrictions

Now that you have the member forms completed, the information verified, and a list compiled for the official directory, you have created a party pool. Only members will have access to the directory (unless you are planning a fund-raiser and want additional exposure to pump up the funds). Once the directories have been printed and distributed, get ready for the big splash made by those diving into your party pool.

Chips and Tips

When members are willing to share a skill or talent that is in their actual line of work, their commitment (per occasion) should be limited to an hour or two gratis and perhaps, at a discount after that.

Party Pool by the Rules

The rules for this pool do not prohibit horseplay, yelling, glass containers, or pets. Nor are the hours restricting. In fact, the more of the above, the better the party. However, there are a few rules to observe.

In Plan No. 1, making arrangements to utilize another's equipment and skills is between the individuals. No record will be kept of the activity. It is each member's job to keep track of his own participation and if unable to comply, just say no.

Festive Facts

When planning a hockey banquet, the moms tapped into their party pool for almost all of their supplies, decorations, and entertainment. This stretched their event budget to include a ticket to an NHL game for each member of the team.

Plan No. 2 involves a simple bookkeeping system in which all uses of services or equipment are recorded. Each member receives credits or debits to his account. Members may charge small fees if they feel it necessary, for material or maintenance expenses.

Paying Off the Pool

Party pooling can expand your resources immensely with a surge of expertise and support. The party pool concept brings to its members an enthusiasm and anticipation that may start them on a whirl of home entertaining.

With the shared-hosting options covered in this chapter, from the most basic to the very complex, you can have a team to help you succeed with a splash. When you jump into your party pool, you'll never again get in over your head.

The Least You Need to Know

- Set ground rules when you first build your party pool.
- A list of members, services and their "out-of-pool" expenses makes up a directory.
- One person can start the pool, and others jump in along the way.
- A team of party helpers can greatly relieve party hosting stress.

Chapter 5

When It's Time to Go Pro

In This Chapter

- Deciding when you need to hire a professional
- Knowing how to read a contract
- Hiring a caterer
- Photographers for moving or still pictures
- Entertainment for all

Just by reading this book you will hone your party skills and gain confidence to throw any party you choose. However, there may be times when you feel the need to get expert help in planning, catering, decorating, entertainment, or photographing your special event. You might make this decision because you don't have the time to do the work yourself, or you just need an expert to make sure everything is done right.

When hiring an expert, your first option is to seek the recommendations of friends and family. Find out the names of suppliers they have hired or seen in action. Unfortunately, though, that isn't always going to be possible, but when it isn't, your only resource is the phone book or Internet. You will want to have the right questions ready, so that in your search you can make the perfect choice of a reputable, experienced, and suitable party professional.

Going Pro with Style

You've been planning your party for months, but realize that you need someone to oversee the actual event, make the food, entertain your guests, or just take photographs. The question isn't how to find these people, but how to find the *proper* people for your party.

The best way to find the right professional is through word of mouth. Ask friends, family, or co-workers—anyone you trust for recommendations on the right professional for you.

If you've asked around and you still come up blank, there are some ways you can find vendors to work with. First, try contacting professional associations that potential suppliers may belong to. Most have a standard of professional practice to ensure that you are dealing with an event professional.

Chips and Tips

Call your favorite restaurant to see if you might be able to get someone to freelance for you. Often your regular waitperson will be free to help you at your party.

In Appendix B, "Party-Planning Product and Service Resources," you'll find a resource list full of information on professional associations, as well as qualified books and Web sites that might help you get started.

Once you have identified a professional you think you would like to work with, the next step is to interview each potential vendor in person, preferably at their place of business. If you are trying to set up an appointment and the vendor resists meeting in person, you might as well cross him or her off your list. Something fishy is probably going on. A true professional won't mind meeting you in their office or at the party venue. If they won't meet you, it's possible the vendor is running a fly-by-night operation.

Here is a list of questions to ask the vendor during an interview:

1. How many years have you been in business? (If the person is just starting out, that is not necessarily a problem. Check if the vendor has a strong education or has similar work experience with another company.)
2. How many years have you been at this location?
3. Are you insured with a liability policy with a minimum of $1 million worth of coverage? (If so, you would like to be put on the insurance certificate as an additional insured. If not, find another vendor.)
4. What happens in case of equipment breakdown? (If it's not already on-site, backup equipment should be available to be delivered to the site immediately in case of an emergency.)

5. In case of an illness, who will take the place of a vendor?
6. When do you need a final count? (This question is for caterers.)
7. Who are three clients whom I may contact who have had a similar event to mine in the last year? (If you are booking someone to handle a wedding, their experience doing a corporate holiday party is not going to give you an apples-to-apples comparison. You want referrals with like parties.)
8. What are your professional affiliations?
9. How do I make my final payment? Cash? Personal check? Bank check? Credit card? (Do not pay in cash until the event is over to your satisfaction. Otherwise, pay by check or credit card.)
10. How long before the event may I cancel without penalty? (The farther away you are from the event when you cancel, the less in penalties you should be charged.

Oftentimes, vendors will supply you with letters of recommendation. Do not allow these letters to substitute for calling referrals directly. By getting personal with someone, you are much more likely to get the real scoop.

And finally—and most importantly—request a printed bid or estimate. The promptness, thoroughness, or professionalism with which they respond is your first clue to their business expertise and performance.

Signing a Consultant on the Dotted Line

Special event coordinator, party planner, event specialist, wedding consultant—whatever you call him or her, this is the person you will hire to be your party "safety net." Jump in and enjoy, because this professional will see to it that everything will be planned the way you want it.

Your planner could assist you with your entire event or just one or more portions of it. It is even possible to hire an *on-site manager* who will, after one or two consultation meetings, show up on the big day and coordinate the event from setup to teardown.

Shindig Sayings

An **on-site manager** is someone who will show up on the day of your event to coordinate and oversee everything from the setup to the teardown and cleanup.

A professional consultant will work with vendors of your choosing or make recommendations from her known "performers" to make up the ideal team for your needs. There are big advantages to working with a coordinator's preferred suppliers, those

Chips and Tips

An event planner who has earned the designation of CSEP (Certified Special Events Professional) has achieved a rigorous set of qualifications and passed extensive testing given by George Washington University in association with the International Special Events Society (www.ISES.com). Certified planners are considered the best in their field. If your selected planner does not currently have the designation, check if they are working toward becoming certified.

with whom there is an established long-term relationship.

While the fee you pay a planner, by the job or by the hour, may seem high, the services he or she offers are invaluable. In fact, since planners often receive professional discounts not available to the consumer, his or her fee might be absorbed in the savings you make using the discount. Plus, since the planner works at this every day, he or she has access to unique, hard-to-find resources and suppliers that will add unforgettable touches to your event.

An experienced planner will help implement the details, protect your interests, and determine the timing needed to make your event pull together, without flaw. For example, he or she will contract and reconfirm deliveries and setups to make sure that every piece of the party design is put in place. Good news! A planner's job can also include cleaning up at party's end, when you are too pooped to "un-party." This type of careful and comprehensive coordination, along with expert scheduling, gives you the luxury of enjoying your party—as much or more than your guests.

Whose party is this, anyway? It is important that you find a coordinator who shares your vision and will enhance and implement it rather than impose his or her own concept. The ideal planning partner will offer creative ideas that will help you stay within your budget or perhaps be more imaginative, and at the same time, strive to lead you to your desired party plan.

In other words, get a complete list of what, when, and how your plan will be carried out and exactly what and when you will be expected to pay. If you are hiring the planner for just parts of your event, you must get a list of details that will be your responsibility to complete. Leave none of this to doubt.

A Catered Affair

When your event calls for something far more substantial or elaborate than chips and dip, and your cooking skills are more along the lines of opening a can and heating the contents thoroughly, you might want to consider hiring a caterer.

Even if you are a fantastic cook, there may be occasions when hiring a professional is a good idea. Are you feeding the masses, and are your cooking facilities limited? Perhaps the menu is complicated and you would be too busy preparing and serving the meal. Whatever your reason—necessity or luxury—hiring a catering service might be just the needed ingredient for your party's success.

For larger parties, many caterers bring full kitchens equipped to prepare elaborate menus for you and your guests. If your party is smaller, your caterer might even prepare food in your kitchen, but for the most part, will bring it ready-to-serve. Some set up kitchens in tractor trailers, while others create a kitchen under a tent in your yard. There will be times the caterer will commandeer your garage, or simply pull up into your driveway with a real chuck wagon and serve up a feast for your cowhands.

Chips and Tips

You can get a referral to find a caterer from the National Association of Catering Executives 708-480-9080 or www.nace.net.

Should you need to rent items like dishes, glasses, and flatware, you may want to make a trip to the rental store to get into the swing of planning your party. Good party-rental stores will offer a wide variety of styles to suit your style, tastes, and theme of your event.

Festive Facts

While a cowboy was out on the trail driving cattle, his world revolved around the chuck wagon. Made from a Civil War army-surplus wagon, the chuck wagon was built to hold food and other supplies for the cowboys. Driven by the cook, the chuck wagon traveled in front of cowboys and carried not only their food, but also cooking supplies and even extra guns, personal items, or musical instruments.

However, if you are short on time or are not sure what you want, your caterer, with care and expertise, will make choices that will be superb. In order to keep up with competition, successful caterers are prepared to set up incredibly beautiful tables with yours, theirs, or rented linens and serving containers. Many keep warehouses of their own stock to only be used at parties they cater.

Whether you decide to do the cooking yourself or have food simply delivered, one of the best investments you can make for your party's success is to hire a wait staff for last-minute preparations. They will also serve the food, clear dishes during the party, and be in charge of postparty cleanup. Most caterers will be happy to send experienced servers to do their miracles, but there's nothing wrong in hiring your own children or those of your friends.

Shindig Sayings

An **open or hosted bar** means that guests are not expected to pay for any of the drinks available at the bar. An open bar can last the duration of the night, or for a set time period.

Total bar setup is another party service that your caterer can provide. This may be as uncomplicated as sending over a portable bar and bartender and using your liquor, or as complete as allowing you to use their stock for a by-the-drink price at an *open or hosted bar* (guests can order any drink available in the bar selection) during a set time period.

Once you've had a chance to review your caterer's menus and have settled on something (or at least narrowed it down), ask for a food tasting of all the dishes. While you are at it, ask if you may peek into an event comparable to yours, to see a sample of his or her work in action.

It is always a good idea to determine whether or not the staff will be the *"first line"* or will *"add-on"* help be used. In some cases you might want to meet with the person who will be in charge of your party, since this isn't always the boss.

Chips and Tips

Caterers, like most vendors, have their specialties. When calling, make sure to ask what it is. The answer could rescue you from hiring the wrong company for your needs.

Say "Cheese"

What is worse than not taking photographs of your wonderful party? Well, how about taking tons of incredible photos but, unfortunately, your camera jammed somewhere around Photo No. 4 and the rest are ruined? That, dear host, is the reason for Party Rule No. 1: Hire a professional to document your once-in-a-lifetime special occasions.

Sure, your best friend might be a master at taking great shots with his Brownie, instant, or disposable camera, but for images that are first-rate, whether candid or well-posed, be sure to include a professional photographer in your budget.

A professional photographer will not only know all the ins and outs of lighting, shadows, film exposures, settings, composition, and making people relaxed and looking their best, but will also know the tricks and tactics used in developing film that will result in photos destined to be cherished heirlooms.

Chips and Tips

You can find a list of photographers from the International Freelance Photographers Association (www.aipress.com).

Remember, quality photographers carry a variety of cameras with them to capture the best images. Plus, they usually have the backup equipment to ensure that you will have pictures of your event despite camera failure.

Shindig Sayings

A **first line** staff member is someone who works for the caterer on a regular basis and knows the caterer's needs and expectations, while an **add-on** is someone who is used by this caterer on only an occasional basis or who may never have worked for this caterer before.

As with any other professional, choose a photographer who has experience in the type of work you want. If your party is casual and free-flowing, you will be looking for good, semi-posed group shots. In this case, a serious portrait photographer may not have the personality to get guests to act and interact comfortably. Costume parties require a prom or wedding photographer to get those posed yet relaxed shots, and for a family portrait it takes yet another expertise. Skim through sample albums to find the type of photos you would like to have.

Instead of just looking through photo albums, why not ask to visit your photographer during an event shoot, to observe his style and methods? Take special care to note if he or his equipment is obtrusive. Was he dressed appropriately? Did his subjects seem relaxed, and did they smile easily for the photographer? And whatever you do, don't let anything be a substitute for getting personal recommendations from past clients. These people can be your very best source of information.

Party Pitfall

When looking through a photographer's album, be wary of blurry shots or shots where the subjects don't look happy. Taking a great picture means a lot more than just finding a great pose.

And before signing any contract, make sure that you like the photographer. It is going to be awfully hard to smile if you bristle at everything he says or every joke he makes.

While you might find a professional photographer essential to your needs, do provide your guests with disposable cameras to take the casual, informal shots. This will guarantee that you see what is happening in every corner of the party, even when you weren't there. To ensure that guests get the point of the cameras, leave a camera on the table with a note attached which reads: "Take your turn at snapping photos of the guests at the table and other Kodak moments."

Just because you are supplying cameras, don't rely on these to be your only photographs. Remember, when you are making memories of a lifetime, always choose a professional.

Festive Facts

Fred was hosting a family reunion at his house and wanted to capture all those generations on film. To do so, he hired a photographer for family-group photos, strictly based on the man's work samples. Unfortunately, when the photos came back, they were nothing like those seen in the albums. Had he checked customer feedback first, he would have learned that the studio office was always in chaos and that most photos were delayed for weeks, or worse yet, lost forever. And he wouldn't have lost a precious keepsake of the reunion.

They're Moving Pictures, So Move!

What a professional photographer accomplishes with still shots, a trained *videographer* can achieve with video images. Their editing skills can produce a tight collection of video images that tell the story of your party in an interesting manner.

The rules of hiring a videographer are almost the same as hiring a photographer. They also have specialty areas, whether it's weddings, graduations, or children, so be sure to view several reels of their work at events similar to your own. Make certain, too, that you check their references and have a rapport with the videographer. If he or she doesn't make you feel relaxed, the images he or she shoots will show it.

Chips and Tips

Some photographers will come to your event, take the photos, and leave the film for you to develop. The savings in this agreement over purchasing prints is considerable.

And just as you might with a photographer, it is important to see the videographer in action. Attend one or more functions similar to yours. Even if these are private parties, you can sometimes inconspicuously attend and observe.

When checking over your contract, be sure to note who will be taking the video. Is it the person you actually met with or an assistant? This could make all the difference in what your final video looks like, and is definitely worth noting in the contract.

Design Team

Your dream is to transform your home into the Taj Mahal. Chances are you won't find all the materials you need to accomplish that at your local party store. That's where an event designer comes in. A good designer will turn your dream into a visual reality. Like a set designer for a play or movie, an event designer will build props and supply furnishings to capture the mood and theme you desire. Good designers are also masters of illusion. They can create items using lightweight and portable materials that will turn canvas into marble and Styrofoam into stone, all so realistic looking you would have to touch them to realize they weren't real.

Shindig Sayings

Unlike a photographer who uses still images, a **videographer** uses moving pictures to tell a story. He or she usually has the skill to not only film the event, but edit the tape to a more interesting format and length than you would be able to do.

Designers will work with all the members of your party team to create plans for every aspect of the party, from the sign-in tables to the buffet tables, from the dining room to the powder room. These talented artists are limited only by your budget and imagination. However, even with a limited budget, the right designer will know where and how to spend the allotted dollars to achieve the best effect for your vision.

Party Pitfall

To avoid guests walking off with disposable cameras at the end of the party, set out a basket bearing a sign, "Leave cameras here," near the exit as a reminder.

Event designers often have specialties. While there are a number of people who have a wide range of designs, you will more likely find that some specialize in wedding designs, while still another does business theater or bar/bat mitzvahs. If possible, ask to see not only the sketches and notes for an event similar to yours, but also photos of how the plan turned into the final party design.

Chips and Tips

Many professional videographers are members of the Wedding & Event and Videographers Association International (www.weva.com).

If you have limited size, time, or budget constraints, your designer or planner can also arrange for less-elaborate effects which will be centered around the dining and buffet tables. Different themes will be achieved through the use of table settings, linens, chair covers, centerpieces, and miscellaneous themed pieces.

Festive Facts

Many designers started out working for an interior design firm or a theater and worked their way into the event industry. Most have warehouses filled with props that can be used and reused for a number of events.

Chips and Tips

If you are having trouble verbalizing your vision, try to share pictures cut from magazines or clipped in books that have the feel of the effect you are hoping to achieve.

Chips and Tips

Contact the American Rental Association (www.ARARental.org or 1-800-334-2177) for their member's stores in your area.

Another option for the budget conscious is a qualified balloon artist. The balloon industry has come a long way from blowing up some balloons and hanging them from the ceiling, or filling up a bunch of balloons with helium and placing them helter-skelter around the room. Today's balloon artists take classes, belong to associations, and even go to conferences where other artists from around the world gather to exchange ideas and designs.

Using a variety of products, balloon artists can build walls of color, write out messages, drape a ceiling, create sculptures made up entirely of latex and Mylar balloons, or arrange for hundreds of balloons to drop at a given time on your guests' heads.

The right designer can help make all your party fantasies come true, at a budget you can afford. Just make sure to check any references that might be made available to you.

If You Can't Buy It ... Rent It

There undoubtedly will be times when you will host a party that has more than eight or twelve guests—the standard size for dinner place settings. When those times occur, head to your local rental store. There you will find a wide variety of dishes, glasses, serving pieces, silverware, and even linens that will fit any table size. And speaking of tables, rental stores also carry different-sized tables and carry chairs—folding or padded, metal or wood. Many rental businesses even carry child-sized table and chair sets.

A good rental store is the place to find things like tents, candlesticks, portable bars, chafing dishes, punch bowls ... anything you would need to pull off a special event.

Even with a signed contract, it is always a good idea to call the rental store a week before the event, just to ensure that they are aware of the delivery and all the items contracted for.

Party Pitfall

When your rental items are picked up, or delivered, do not sign the acceptance receipt until you have counted and examined each item. If there are missing, damaged, or permanently stained items, you need to mark it down on your receipt. Otherwise, you will be charged substantial replacement fees after the event.

Let Me Entertain You

The party is set, the guests have arrived, they are dazzled by the decor, and their mouths are watering at the first taste of the exceptional cuisine—and the party just flops. Why? Because at a party for young business professionals, you chose to ask your cousin to play "Lady of Spain" on his accordion while your niece tap dances.

You've probably been to many parties where your host feels that his CD collection, no matter how sparse, is sufficient entertainment. How many minutes was it before you "remembered" that your grandmother was in a coma and you had to run?

Chips and Tips

Save money by asking friends to bring their favorite CDs. That will help ensure that you are always playing music at least one of them likes.

The type of entertainment planned for a party doesn't have to be elaborate, but it should be appropriate to the event. For instance, you wouldn't plan a Mexican fiesta with an Israeli dance troupe. By the same token, you shouldn't bring in a rap group to entertain a group of senior citizens. Choose the entertainment type to suit your theme, guest list, and surroundings.

Besides music, try thinking of other forms of entertainment. You might hire celebrity look-alikes for a movie-theme event. How about sketch artists or caricaturists for an art theme? Highland dancers would be good for a St. Patrick's Day party, while a New Orleans-style jazz band would be just right for a Mardi Gras gathering.

Since it's difficult to find the exact entertainers you need from the phone book, work with a reliable talent agent, or let your event planner obtain the proper performers for you.

Before You Sign on the Dotted Line

Before you sign any contract, make sure it contains these provisions and that you understand all aspects of the contract. If necessary, have your attorney review any paperwork.

These provisions should appear on all contracts:

- The types of services rendered
- Times of arrival and departure
- Event date, time and location
- Set-up and tear down schedule, if applicable
- Fee-payment schedule including overtime fees
- Cancellation policies
- Liability insurance in place for a minimum of $1 million naming you as an additional insured for the duration of your event
- Contact information during and after business hours
- Sales tax, if any
- Additional labor or equipment fees
- Inclement weather provisions, if applicable
- Power, lighting, gas and/or water requirements, if applicable
- Set up and clean-up fees, if applicable
- Meals provided and break schedules, if applicable
- Dressing area, if necessary
- Attire, if applicable
- Back-up equipment, if applicable
- Who is responsible for obtaining and paying for any permits, if necessary

Look for these additional items on an event planners contract.

- Liability—if decor items are rented or owned by planner, who is contracting with vendors (you or the planner)
- Who is responsible for negotiating all vendor contracts—you or the planner
- Who will pay the vendors—you or the planner, per-hour or per-job cost
- Replacement fee on lost or damaged rental items

When hiring a caterer, check the contract for these additional types of services rendered:

- Liability— or replacement fees if items are rented
- Trash-disposal provisions
- Disposal of leftovers
- Per-person or per-job cost

When hiring a photographer, look for these additional clauses in your contract:

- The number of photos taken
- Per-hour, per-photo, or per-job cost
- Cost of photo duplication
- Types and sizes of final photographs
- Special effects on photos
- Due date of final album
- Who owns the proof sheets, negatives or proof photos
- Photo copyrights

When hiring a videographer, look for these additional clauses to your contract:

- How many hours of raw footage will be shot
- Per-hour, per-job cost
- Cost of videotape duplication
- Format of final product
- Special effects on the final edited reel
- Due date of final edited reel
- Who owns the raw footage
- Copyrights

If hiring a decor designer, look for these additional provisions to the standard contract:

- If decor items are rented or owned
- Replacement fee on lost or damaged rental items

The Least You Need to Know

- Never hire someone unless you've had a chance to interview him or her in person first.
- When hiring a caterer, be sure you get a chance to sample every item from the menu before signing the contract.
- Always make sure to see samples of any professional's work before finalizing an agreement and ask for referrals of clients who have had events similar to yours.
- Be sure to call all professionals a week before the event to confirm details.

Part 2

To Party Means to Plan

Wouldn't it be great if you could throw the best party anyone has ever seen without doing any work? Sure it would be great, but then everyone would be doing it. Throwing a great party means working at it. You need to plan a theme, set your budget (and stick to it), and, of course, invite your guests.

Many people shy away from throwing parties because planning them seems like too much work. Now it is your turn to move out of the ranks of the party fearful to the party fearless. Read on to discover how easy it can be to stock a bar, what it takes to make fancy and fun invitations, and how to make even the smallest apartment large enough to hold a bash your guests will never forget.

Chapter 6

The Theme Says It All

In This Chapter

- Determining a theme
- Looking at your home's decor to establish a theme
- Hobbies make great theme parties
- Following your theme through from the invitations to the good-byes

Birthday or anniversary, barbecue or tea party, formal or casual—whatever the celebration or its style, adding a theme can add excitement and personality to your parties. A theme adds a dimension to events that most gatherings lack. It brings up the level of interest and unites the guests before the day of the party with a common excitement.

In this chapter you'll learn how to give a boring, everyday party pizzazz just by adding a theme. You'll learn how to excite your guests with theme invitations, decorations, and even food.

Is a Theme Necessary?

Is a theme necessary for you to host a successful celebration? Perhaps not. Desirable? Let's explore that. Here are two party examples—you choose the party to which you would prefer to go.

1. **Party 1**

   You go to your mailbox and find a store-bought party invitation. It's a standard greeting card with a balloon design imprinted on the front. You open it, and handwritten in the very small spaces provided, it says: "We're Having a Party!" It gives the names of the host, address, phone number, and date.

   Handwritten on the back of the card (because there is no proper place provided to write it), it reads: "We want to show off the videos of our trip to China. Hope you can make it. Dress is casual. Buffet and cocktails will be served."

   Ho-hum.

2. **Party 2**

   Your doorbell rings. When you open the door, your letter carrier hands you a cardboard mailer (a Chinese take-out box). The carton, trimmed with large Chinese lettering, has on it a shiny red label in the shape of a dragon that bears your name and address. You open it and there you find a fortune cookie, tea bag, and a colorful paper fan along with an invitation printed on a postcard of the Great Wall of China. The invitation reads: "Join us for video highlights of our journey to the mysterious Orient, along with cocktails and a *Szechwan, Mandarin,* and *Cantonese* buffet supper. We begin our journey down the Yangtzee River at 8 P.M. on Saturday, January 20, 2001. Call 989-555-2938 by January 10 to reserve your place in our pagoda. Mandarin garments encouraged. Bill and Nancy Smith."

Shindig Sayings

Many of the foods in **Mandarin** cuisine are wheat, instead of rice-based, consisting of dumplings, breads, and noodles. The food is mild in taste.

Cantonese food is the mildest and most common kind of Chinese food.

Szechwan food is liberal in the use of garlic, scallions, and chilies on chicken, pork, and seafood.

Now, which party would you rather attend?

The first example is the way we are usually invited to parties. It's functional … but boring. From the invitation, you know you will spend an evening watching home movies from your friend's recent trip. These occasions have a boredom stigma and are often successful as a cure for insomnia.

The second one immediately tells you this is going to be an interesting party. In fact, if the party lives up to the magic of the invitation, it's going to be unforgettable. This has to be more than a boring evening watching home movies. A party like this will not only be memorable, but possibly educational and definitely exciting.

Now, isn't that the way you'd want your guests to look forward to all of your parties?

In the case of the second party, your friends have not only sent out a unique invitation, but have chosen to wrap the entire party around a Chinese theme. It makes perfect sense. The films are of their trip to China, they probably have brought back interesting souvenirs, and it's an easy theme to carry through. Why not make the experience of watching the video as exciting for their friends as taking the trip was for them?

Sometimes choosing a theme is not as obvious, and you will be required to use a little creative imagination when coming up with your theme.

Let the Occasion Set the Theme

Chances are, you have already held a number of parties with simple themes. Have you ever purchased birthday party goods imprinted with "Over the Hill," or a golf design, or scenes from a nursery rhyme? Those are themes.

You can make any holiday event extraordinary by expanding on a theme. For example, "Trim a Tree" or "Carve a Pumpkin" are very common themes for Christmas and Halloween. However, you can make a simple holiday party unique by taking the typical holiday and adding a twist—"Pilgrim's Turkey Trot" or "Stars and Stripes Triathlon." By giving these holidays another added dimension—ragtime dancing and sports—you have made a mundane holiday memorable.

Sometimes if you just move the routine date of an event, it is enough to create a festive atmosphere that brands it truly special. If you want, host a "Christmas in July," or in May have an "Every Night Is New Year's Eve" theme party for a person who adores the holiday season.

You see, you don't have to create something new, you just have to move it out of context to make it reappear in an exciting way.

Kids' Play

Kids' parties are usually theme-related. In fact, there is a huge industry devoted to designing preprinted party goods of a favorite cartoon or comic character, sports, dolls, space travel, or other child-friendly subjects. It is so easy to buy these products. Just go into the store or an online vendor and pick out every item that's in a particular line.

The problem is that while such party goods are festive, they are also perhaps too familiar or common for some people.

Crafty parents will often produce extremely individualized themes for their children's parties by creating their own invitations, decorations, costumes, favors, and fun foods. When this is the case, the whole family often joins in to make a party of preparing for the party.

There is nothing wrong in buying prepackaged theme designs. They can be very helpful if you feel your skills are lacking or you're just short of time. However, with very little effort, you can still make these party packages more personal and unique.

Parties by Design

Why should the kids get to have all the fun? There's no reason that big kids can't hold a theme party with a little more adult pizzazz—not when there are so many ways of shaking things up and coming up with a fabulous bash. Shouldn't a 60th anniversary party, planned for a couple who were wed during the big band era, swing? Or how about basing a graduation celebration for a finance student around the trappings of big business and Wall Street?

You can invent your theme by looking around your surroundings. This is particularly effective when you are starting out because it means you don't have to fight your decor—you work with it. It's very difficult to hold a *Lost in Space* party when you are surrounded by furniture that looks as if it belongs in a ranch house in Texas. You can do it, of course, but it takes a lot more work and money to transform it. Why fight it? Look at your furniture. Even if it's a mishmash, chances are there is at least one style that stands out. Let the design decide the feeling for the event, then all you have to do is create a theme to suit the occasion and the surroundings.

Festive Facts

An eager hostess invited her guests to celebrate her new washing machine at an impromptu all-white dinner party. Within hours she had tumbled together a menu, table decor, and party favors for her "blanc" bash. Getting into the spirit, the guests dressed in white and brought small gifts like detergent, bleach, and softeners, for the new "occupant."

It's a Grand Old Flag

Is your decor Early American? You can plan a colonial party featuring Yankee pot roast and flags on display to honor Betsy Ross, the creator of the first American flag. Then hold a rousing sing-along of patriotic songs. If it's not a general celebration but a milestone birthday, give the theme a patriotic plug such as "He's a Grand Old Man."

Festive Facts

In June 1776, Betsy Ross was a brave widow struggling to run her own upholstery business. Upholsterers in colonial America not only worked on furniture, but did all manner of sewing work, which included making flags. According to accounts given by Betsy Ross, General Washington came to her home and showed her a rough design of the flag that included a six-pointed star. Betsy, a standout with the scissors, demonstrated how to cut a five-pointed star in a single snip. Impressed, George Washington entrusted Betsy with making our first flag.

Futuristic Festivities

Is your furniture style high-tech? If so, a futuristic celebration would be more appropriate. Show off all your technological devices and set them up against your chrome and glass furniture. You and your guests can play virtual or video games. Serve freeze-dried cuisine, like the meals eaten by astronauts, or have guests place their dinner orders online or via a fax. This atmosphere would be ideal for a graduation, retirement, engagement, or going-away party with the title, "Here's to Your Future." High-tech styles also work well with "Man of the New Millennium" or *Star Trek* theme parties.

Using Your Surroundings

Wicker and rattan furniture will set the scene for a luau, beach party, or some oriental themes.

Likewise, a Danish Modern setting calls for a *smorgasbord,* while an English Tudor is perfect for either a formal dinner with Beef Wellington or set up as a lively pub complete with fish and chips and dart games.

Shindig Sayings

A **smorgasbord** is a Scandinavian buffet offering a variety of hot and cold foods.

If your home is made up of a wide variety of differing styles too numerous to define, then use this to your advantage. Create a "Pieces of My Life" party and tag each item that has a great story: "Found at Goodwill thrift shop for $5 a week after I left home" or "Picked out of my neighbor's garbage late one night." Neither you nor your guests will ever again look at your furnishings without smiling at the memories.

If you want to narrow your eclectic surroundings down further, look around your home and see if there is one focal point that draws everyone's attention. Is your living room dominated by a grand piano? A concert, cabaret, or piano bar party is the perfect choice. Use sheet music, books, or musical instruments to accent this theme.

When there is an important event happening, does everyone come to your place to watch your large-screen TV? You can be the producer of a theme party around a televised event like the Academy Awards, the Grammys, or the Superbowl. Let the focal point of your home be the kick-off point for a black-tie-and-gown awards soiree or a sports spuds-and-suds day.

As you can see, any type of surroundings or focal point can be made to work to your advantage and turned into a theme.

Home Is Where I Hang My Hat

If looking at the inside of your home doesn't inspire you, look outside.

Live in an apartment building? You can pretend it is a high-rise penthouse. Get a friend to act as a door attendant outside your building to greet and usher in your guests. Make it a very chic and avant-garde event set in New York's *SoHo*. Or pretend you live in the notorious Dakota apartments across the street from Central Park and home to the late John Lennon and the site of *Rosemary's Baby*. Consider the possibilities. What other stories can that building tell? Uptown or downtown, this theme will give your parties a new lease.

Festive Facts

SoHo is a New York City neighborhood named after its location, **SO**uth of **HO**uston Street. SoHo is famous for the old industrial buildings that grace its streets and for the shops, galleries, and artists who reside there.

Do you live out on the farm or in the country? You can have a party at your homestead that will allow for some real stretching out. Outdoor locations lend themselves to casual themes like:

- "Westward Ho" (urban cowboy, Tex-Mex, cattle drive, barbecue)
- "State Fair" (if your friends can fruits, raise animals, grow vegetables—any activities you'd find at a State Fair—show them off at this party)

- "Take a Break by the Lake" (terrific for having everyone come over for a dip in your own private swimming hole)

Guests can enjoy everything from volleyball to horseback riding in wide-open spaces. If you are lucky enough to live in the country, let it be the scheme for your theme.

Love Will Keep Us Together

There is really no limit to taking a typical celebration and giving it some sizzle. When it comes to anniversary parties, there is a good plan for any year, from the first to the 75th. You might pick the couple's wedding song as the central theme or trace their life together via several song titles: "We've Only Just Begun," "She's Having My Baby," "Sunrise, Sunset," "Love Will Keep Us Together," and "I Would Still Choose You."

Here are some ways to choose your themes based on personal information about the happy couple.

1. Select the ballads of a favorite singer of the celebrating couple, or pick the music of a particular era that is meaningful to your guests of honor. Romance, nostalgia, and sentiment can be created by playing "their song."
2. Where did they meet? For a 50th anniversary couple, replicate their favorite restaurant and the meal they enjoyed on their first date. Print a menu from that year with authentic prices, charge the guests for their dinner, and present the cash to the couple for a special meal—at today's prices.

Chips and Tips

If you are throwing a party for someone, you most likely know them very well; however, if you don't, contact his or her family or best friends to ask them about the habits and haunts of the guest of honor to help you with your theme selection.

Couples about to be married or wed from a few years to several decades will be thrilled with such thoughtful celebrations and will cherish the memories through their lifetime together.

Leisure Pursuits

Symbols of hobbies, pastimes, and talents are great bases for a theme party. Have you been collecting comic books for a lifetime? Then why not hold a superhero party? (You will be surprised at how many adult men will be attracted to this theme.) This is a party strong in primary colors and whimsy (see Chapter 23, "From Tots to Teens—Total Party Plans").

Your passion for gardening will bloom in a "Ladies for Lunch" garden party. Use homegrown flowers, plants, and produce (see Chapter 18, "Spring Flings").

Is he hot-wired to ESPN's all-sports coverage? Then a gridiron idea is the perfect party plan (see Chapter 23).

By the Book

When you walk into your friend's home and it's filled floor to ceiling with books, you've got your theme right there. If novels are to his liking, scan his bookshelves for likely inspiration. Perhaps he has the entire *Hardy Boys* or John Grisham collection? It doesn't take a detective to analyze the evidence that he would love being feted at a mystery party.

Check out their bookshelves and see if you can determine a pattern.

1. *Gone with the Wind* fan? This theme begs for mint juleps, fresh flowers, fried chicken, and southern hospitality. Your guests will gather on the verandah and party as if there's no tomorrow (see Chapter 19, "The Heat Is On").
2. Would she die for *Dracula?* Ghastly friends will "suck up" to you for an invitation to celebrate your "ghost of honor" (see Chapter 20, "Fall Festivities").

Getting the idea? There are almost as many themes as there are book titles.

Chips and Tips

Go to secondhand stores or garage sales to buy copies of old books. Use them as favors or decorations.

Chips and Tips

The most important rule for deciding upon a theme is to consider the guest of honor and his or her personality, interests, talents, pastimes, and goals. You'll find the ideal theme for celebrating a person, and there is no better honor.

Couch Potato Chips

Just like a book party, you can easily make the same plans for the couch potato and his favorite TV shows, or the film fan and her selection of video picks. Familiarize yourself with your friend's habits and hobbies for clues to the theme party that would be a good fit.

Pastime Parties

Virtually any hobby can be adapted to a theme party. Bugs, bats, or birds—whatever your friend's pastime pursuits, you can create a theme that showcases what he or she loves.

A Combination of Sights and Delights

For people who love to travel or someone with strong ethnic ties, theme parties with an international flair are the ticket. However, to give a generic international subject a twist, you can combine themes to create other variations. For example, if you choose a gambling theme, add some international adventure by setting the casino in Monte Carlo.

1. A beach party is invariably fun, but it takes on a down under dimension when you "put another shrimp on the *barbie*" for an Australian soiree. G'day, mates!
2. A trip into The Twilight Zone can be your party theme with the addition of fortune-tellers; palm, tarot-card, and tea-leaf readers; handwriting analysts; and psychic messages from beyond.

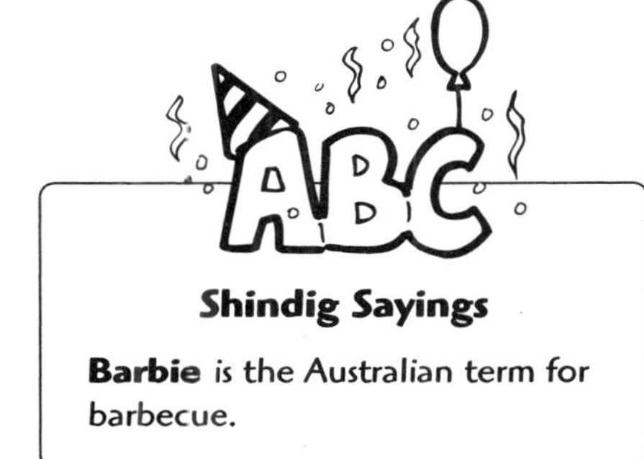

Shindig Sayings

Barbie is the Australian term for barbecue.

Pack your party plan and treat your worldly (and otherworldly) guests to an imaginary trip. No matter what your destination, your guests will love you for going that extra mile.

Time Tunnel

If you are brainstorming ideas, don't forget to look back in time to celebrate past eras. There were cakewalks and ice cream socials at the turn of the twentieth century. The 1920s brought prohibition, flappers, and bathtub gin. The "B-Boys"—Beach Boys and The Beatles—epitomize the styles of the '60s. Take a trip down nostalgia lane. Each decade is a source of theme inspiration.

Alternately, you can zoom ahead into the space age, with themes following leaders like *Star Wars, Star Trek,* and true-life space exploration.

Make Mine with a Twist

Although not really themes, serving styles can be the basis of a party theme. Clam bakes, barbecues, tailgates, potlucks, fish fries, or fondue cooking are among the ways of serving that are quite social and theme inspiring.

Several strategies are also party basics that can be built on. These include scavenger hunts, progressive parties, ongoing parties (like dining or tasting clubs), surprise parties, and housewarming parties. Here, too, you can blend a personalized theme with the strategy for a super event.

Set the scavenger hunt into a Halloween theme where guests have to trick or treat for treasures on their list. Or put the fondue party in a Swiss setting for a tasty trip theme.

Get creative. Explore every avenue available to look for theme inspiration.

Follow Through in All You Do

Finally, if you're still stuck, you can find multiple resources and books for total party plans. For instance, if you're online, check out www.PartyPlansPlus.com for a wide range of events planned from the invitation to the souvenirs.

The key to a successful theme celebration is to follow through. Start with the invitation and make sure you follow the theme with your choices of decor, menu, entertainment, prizes, and souvenirs.

The Least You Need to Know

- A party with a theme gives all of the guests something in common long before they arrive at the party.
- Theme parties give you a path to follow and narrow your choices to make planning simple.
- A theme can be based on almost anything: hobbies, collections, the site, talents, interests, or occupations.
- For best results, incorporate the theme into every element of the party.

Chapter 7

Banking on a Budget

In This Chapter

- Establishing your party budget
- Finding bargain party supplies
- Do-it-yourself solutions

Throwing a party doesn't mean you have to throw your budget out of whack. Although it does require spending some money, it shouldn't mean spending your kid's college funds or your dream vacation savings. That would take a lot of the enjoyment out of planning a party. And we all know that the first rule of throwing a party is for the host to enjoy it!

So, get out your pencil and sharpen it to a fine point while we show you how to prepare a party budget with some clever cost-cutting and money-saving maneuvers.

Rule of Thumb

The party budget rule of thumb is that there is no set rule. Parties and budgets are as individual as the people who throw them. While one host routinely spends $500 on a casual get-together, another might not spend that amount on a year's worth of entertaining. The good news is that, with a little creativity and flexibility, you can spend as much or as little as you can afford and still achieve an outstanding outcome.

Chips and Tips

To save time and error in your master plans, consider using one of the software management programs to track budget items, actual costs, and reminders for special deadlines. Staying on top of expenditures and timelines will prevent party pitfalls.

One of the first things you'll need to consider is the type of party you are having and who will be attending. Casual gatherings with close friends and family usually don't require a large outlay. While formal parties with new acquaintances or business associates may mean you'll want to show off a little more.

Time and Money

Say you have a family birthday and you know that inviting folks over for a barbecue is the easiest and least-expensive way for you to entertain. Since this is a special celebration, however, you want to make it a little more elaborate. You start to think you'll add a few decorations, some simple activities, and perhaps light entertainment to make it more festive. You think, "That won't break the bank." Then after a little checking, you discover that things cost more than you imagined and the tally is mounting.

All of these extras will mean spending more time and money to make things perfect. If your life is busy, time is money, so finding bargains for your fabulous fete could cost a fortune.

So decide if you can afford to hire someone to do it all for you, or if time is tight, will shopping for plates in three stores be worth the dollar or two you'll save.

Chips and Tips

When you are stumped for a product, service, or vendor resource, give your local party store a call for help. A good store will have a file of "festive folks" and will happily share their leads. Don't, however, forget to get other references.

Distributing the Dollars

Depending upon your personal preferences, your budget allocations will vary. For some hosts, the food is paramount, while for others it's the entertainment. Decide what's important to you and plan your budget accordingly.

The following percentages represent a typical distribution of dollars for a party. Yours may vary depending on tastes, preferences, and flexibility.

Beware of Budget Busters

Just when you think you have it all decided and everything is within your budget, the unexpected expense will crop up to throw your budget for a loophole. When this happens (sorry, but it is "when" and not "if"), you will need to have plans B and C ready.

Some examples of *Murphy's Law* budget busters include sales tax, miscalculating postage, unplanned shipping costs, and rush charges for last-minute items you decide you "must" have.

Item	Percentage of Total Budget
Printed pieces: Invitations, thank-you notes, programs, place cards	3 percent
Decorations: Balloons, flowers, banners, props, linens	15 percent
Food and beverages including labor	40 percent
Entertainment, activities	20 percent
Prizes, gifts, favors	3 percent
Rental items	14 percent
Miscellaneous	5 percent

Chic but Cheap Solutions

The best way to save money on your budget is to go cheap. Whether you are hunting for bargain basement prices, scouring garage sales, or just digging in your own basement, you'll find things you can use for your party, before you go and spend thousands of dollars on things like decorations or entertainment.

Chips and Tips

While your goals will dictate how you divvy up your festivity funds, the most important thing to remember is that you can't spend the same buck twice, so keep an eye on the limits. Once you have listed all of your potential expenses on your master budget sheet, decide how you will mete out your money. Alter the budget, and adjust your party pocketbook accordingly.

Bargain Basement Bonanzas

The art of bargain hunting will be a boon to some party hosts. You can search for close-out and discount items, and holiday sale items ranging from dollar-a-yard linens for your elegant table to the penny-a-piece party favors that fill goody bags for your guests.

When purchasing any holiday sale merchandise, think about what it can be used for other occasions during the year. For instance, red items can be used for Christmas, Valentine's Day and patriotic holidays. Think ahead. Buy great items when you can at a good price and save all year.

Shindig Sayings

Murphy's Law says that whenever something can go wrong, it will go wrong.

Hunting Those Bargains

Tracking down illusive party penny savers takes time, but here are some great places to start your search besides local party goods suppliers. Check rental stores for sale of used but good items, thrift shops, discount clubs, flea markets, and garage sales. Or search the Web and check out auctions (www.eBay.com is great) and online merchants such as www.GreatEntertaining.com.

Attack bargain chasing as diligently as you would job hunting. The money you save will be like finding a second income source.

Festive Facts

A hostess in search of a tropical drink glass called the local liquor distributor in desperation. She needed 200 for a champagne taste party, but with a beer budget. The manager had 400 lovely glasses bearing a full-color parrot insignia and only a tiny logo. He sold them all to her at 10 cents each. He even threw in the huge parrot signs that matched. A creative search paid off in ... well, parrots!

Do It Yourself

Sometimes it is better and cheaper to do it yourself. Cooking up a batch of your favorite chili is going to save money over buying a dozen cans, and it will be far more tasty. A quick trip to the farmers' market to gather bunches of flowers and greens will blossom into savings when you arrange them simply yourself.

Another do-it-yourself winner is to enlist the services (and talents) of amateur entertainers and musicians that will work for free or reasonable rates. Many college or high school drama, choral, or orchestra groups will perform at your party for just a donation to their trip or uniform funds. This pleasant entertainment adds a bright touch to your home party.

A Borrower Be

One of the best ways to stretch your savings is through party pooling as discussed in Chapter 4, "Party Pooling: Sharing a Celebration." When you borrow party basics like twinkle lights, tables, chairs, coat racks, linens, serving pieces, or a helium tank, you will drastically reduce your party payouts.

When entertaining the same guests over and again, learn to recycle props. A treasure chest can be used for a pirate party, tropical theme, Peter Pan or "we treasure you" events.

Occasionally your local theater group, department store, supermarket, video store, or movie theater will let you rent or borrow props. Make friends with managers of stores you frequent. Often displays, posters, props, and decorations from store promotions will be yours for the taking.

Chips and Tips

When considering a menu, check recipes closely. If you are going to need to buy a number of specialty ingredients that you won't use again or will go bad before you can use them another time, check out if buying the dish premade might be a more budget-friendly alternative in the long run.

Buried Treasures

Speaking of treasure chests, the most valuable savings may be buried in your cupboards, garage, attic, basement, and closets. Explore these areas with an open mind for unique items that can be used or adapted to fit your party scheme.

Party Pitfall

Audition all entertainment, particularly low-cost or free. Set up an opportunity to listen to your nephew's "nice little band" during rehearsal to make sure they are skilled enough and appropriate. Sometimes you just can't afford "free" entertainment.

Getting Crafty

If you are artistic and crafty, you can save lots of money by using your creations to enhance your party decor. The methods practiced in craft circles are many and varied; the arts-and-craft stores are a mass of possibilities. Crafting can result in party invitations, decorations, costumes, table decor, gifts, and favors. Almost every facet of your party can be coordinated through the world of glue guns, rubber stamps, stencils, beads, feathers, sequins, stickers, Styrofoam, paints, and glitter. All of these can be used to turn trash to treasure.

Chips and Tips

Keep an eye out for party props wherever you go. You never know when the perfect treasure chest is going to pop up.

Chips and Tips

Fashion chair-back covers from men's white dress shirts. Place them on the chair back, front facing away from the table, tie the arms in an attractive knot, add a ribbon bow tie, and with the "shirt off his back," you have a formal, aesthetic presentation.

Head to the library, check the Internet, or do some channel-surfing on your television. There are dozens of programs on local cable access, Discovery, Home & Garden Television, and Lifetime channels. Crafting is an easy way to safe money while creating one-of-a-kind effects that show your artistic talents.

Bring Your Own

B.Y.O.E. (Bring Your Own Everything) would be a very good way to save scads of money on your event, but it may be a little drastic and is definitely a tactless hosting method.

However, potluck can extend to more than just hot dishes or gelatin molds. Guests may be asked to provide paper and plastic food service items, centerpieces or room decorations. The organization of games and activities is a contribution that will help the host immensely. Start your party planning by making a list of those chores you will gladly part with. Then when a guest asks, "Is there anything I can do to help?" You'll be ready.

The Early Bird Beats the Budget

Ordering certain items early also will enable you to take advantage of sales and special promotions, and you won't have to pay additional fees for rush processing or mailing.

One of the biggest unexpected expenses is that of paying top dollar for something because it's ordered at the last minute. This happens when you either forget to buy or reserve something, or you think of something brilliant in the final hours before the event. This is mostly true when the item needs to be shipped or personalized with engraving or imprinting. Whatever the cause, those deadline disasters will eat into your party budget like the guests at the fresh jumbo-shrimp display.

So, if you get that sudden lightning bolt of inspiration for a fantastic addition to your party, try to control your enthusiasm long enough to determine if it will affect the overall party success and how it will affect your budget.

Party Pitfall

A host found an online merchant for 10 outdoor torches at a savings of $2 each over his local party store. To receive them by ground shipping in 5 to 7 days would have cost $8. This still would have saved him $12. However, since he needed them rushed to him in two days, he not only would have been charged $8 more for rush shipping, the merchant also would have charged $10 more for rush handling. In the end it would have cost him $6 more to order them online.

Unless the detail is going to add a big scoop of à la mode to your party pie, pass on the idea.

The budget-balancing act for your party doesn't mean you have to walk a tightrope or act like a tightwad. Plan carefully and, of course, use this book as a safety net.

The Least You Need to Know

- There is no rule of thumb other than your personal preferences.
- Look for hidden expenses whenever you plan a party.
- Decide what's important to you and plan your budget accordingly.
- Shop year-round for party supplies.
- Party bargains are easy to find if you always have your eyes peeled.

Chapter 8

The Honour of Your Company ...

In This Chapter

- ➤ Including all the necessary details in your invitation
- ➤ Putting together a formal invitation
- ➤ Creating funky envelopes
- ➤ Matching your invitation to your party's theme
- ➤ Using the Internet to invite your guests

Since the invitation is the first time your guests will get to see what type of event you are hosting, it is the most important first ingredient to your party's success. In this chapter you'll learn how you can create inviting invitations. Perfect attendance is almost guaranteed as your peruse these invitation inspirations.

Invitation Imperatives

A good invitation is just like a good news story: Its first goal is to cover the five *W*s of who, what, when, where, and why, along with how-tos and other party imperatives.

You'll want to answer these questions in the invitation.

1. Who is throwing the party? Write out the full names of the hosts.
2. What type of party is it? Formal or casual, cocktail or dinner, theme or scheme. Prepare your guests for what they should expect the minute they walk in the door.

3. When is the party? Make sure you tell the day, date, and start and finish times of the event.
4. Where is the party? Give the address, directions, and a map if necessary.
5. Why is the party being held? State the occasion (birthday, anniversary, bon voyage, new baby, etc.) and honoree's name, if applicable.
6. Your how-tos should include how to respond, the dress code, and what to bring if it's a potluck event. Also include a phone number for responses.

Festive Facts

Just recently a stressed-out hostess inadvertently omitted the date from her invitation. This meant that every invited guest was required to call to find out when the event was to be held. Her faux pas may have qualified her as the only hapless hostess in history to receive a prompt 100 percent response.

Shindig Sayings

A **self-mailer** is an invitation printed on heavy stock and folded either in half or in thirds, affixed with a seal, addressed, stamped, and mailed. This can be done to conserve envelopes or as part of the design plan.

Make sure you have someone else review your invitation before sending it out. This will ensure you have included all the necessary information.

Formal or Funky

Your invitation is a forecast of things to come, so make it as accurate as you can by designing it to match your party atmosphere.

An invitation to a very casual affair can be a hand-printed note copied on attractive stationery and sent as a *self-mailer*. Find a pre-printed paper that matches your theme.

For an elegant occasion such as a wedding or formal sit-down dinner, you might consider more elaborate invitations. Whichever invitation you chose, make sure it reflects your style of the event.

A Formal Flare

For elegant events, you'll find numerous sample books of imprinted materials through your printer, card shop, stationery supplier or on-line.

If ordering from a book isn't your style, you can design formal invitations yourself using a desktop-publishing program and quality invitation stock available from specialty-paper companies or office supply stores. Or work with artists from a full-service print shop.

Once you've chosen and proofread your invitations, simply address, stamp and mail.

Party Pitfall

Reply envelopes should always carry the correct postage. It's inappropriate to ask your guests to pay for the return of the response card.

Creative Casual

For a party that isn't so formal, you have the advantage of being able to use your imagination. Remember, sometimes it isn't so much what you say but how you say it.

For an informal celebration, not only can your invitation be imaginative, you are not limited to sending it in an envelope. In fact, almost any nonflammable, nonbreakable object can go directly through the mail if it has a clearly printed label attached and the correct postage affixed. When in doubt, take your proposed container to the post office to be inspected and approved. Don't spend the time and effort preparing a bunch of creative cards if they can't be mailed.

Chips and Tips

Invitations that are 5" to 11½" long, 3½" to 6⅛" high, and 7/1000" to ¼" thick and weigh 1 ounce or under require one first-class postage stamp. Mail that is larger or smaller than these dimensions, or heavier than 1 ounce, should be taken to the post office to determine proper postage.

Handmade envelopes to match your theme will add to the appeal of your invitation. The list of materials that can be used to construct your envelope is almost limitless. They include wallpaper, gift wrap, newspaper, magazine covers, fabric, or even children's artwork.

Message in a Bottle

A handcrafted "Message in a Bottle" invitation would be captivating for even more than just island or tropical parties. Trinkets and symbols of your party theme can accompany the see-through invitation on its journey into your guests' mailboxes.

Party Pitfall

Proper invitations of any kind should never go through a postage meter.

To achieve the effect, recycle a plastic soda, water, or juice bottle. With a bit of crafting and some inexpensive supplies, you can produce an invitation that will get your guests hopping—island hopping, that is.

You also can send invitations in recycled cardboard paper towel tubes, corrugated cartons, plastic bags or cookie tins, to name a few.

Once you have settled on the product of your whimsy, be sure to send yourself a prototype. The sample invitation should be constructed in the exact way as those you are making for your guests so that you can test its travel time and condition upon arrival.

Chips and Tips

Always include an invitation addressed to yourself with the batch to establish that they were posted, the promptness of receipt, and as a souvenir for your party scrapbook.

Party Pitfall

Do not sprinkle confetti, especially the metallic kind, into your invitation envelope. However festive, they are very unwelcome when they fall into a computer keyboard or carpeting.

Innovative and Inventive Invitations

Once you've decided to go with a theme for your next event, it's important you start with the invitation.

Later in the book, in Chapters 17 through 23, you'll see a number of innovative invitation ideas that are matched to themes. Have fun. Let your invitation be the start of the party … weeks before its scheduled to begin.

A(verage) to Z(any) Invitation Gimmicks

Once you've determined that you are going to send out a funky invitation, it's important to expand your creativity to the wording. After all, sending a packet of salsa is great, but also loses its flavor if your wording is formal.

Here's a sample of items you can use to attach to your invitation and their related catchphrases. Keep in mind that groaning is good for you.

- **Eraser:** "Correct me if I'm wrong …"
- **Gum:** "We want 'chew' to come …"
- **Horoscope:** "The stars say there's a party in your future …"
- **Zipper:** "Zip your lip—it's a surprise …"

Check out inexpensive small toys generally used as prizes in cereal, candy boxes, or in souvenir bags for a child's party as likely items to attach to your invitation.

Respond By ...

Most invitations require an *RSVP* or "respond by." While more formal invitations often include a card that needs to be sent back to the host, casual RSVPs can be done by phone.

Shindig Sayings

RSVP stands for *repondez, s'il vous plait* in French ("please respond"). This means that whether guests are attending the party or not, you are asking for a response. Regrets or regrets only means you want to hear only from those guests who will not be attending.

Spreading the Word

The most popular way to send in invitation is through the mail. However, it is important to make sure you mail it out early enough to ensure that people have enough time to hire babysitters, plan costumes, or just get excited. We've put together a list of mailing tips:

- **Milestone occasions:** (weddings, special anniversaries, or milestone birthdays): Send invitations out four to six weeks before the event.
- **Theme or costume parties:** Mail the invitations at least four weeks ahead.
- **Holiday parties:** Invite your guests four to six weeks ahead of the party date, especially if your party is on a Saturday night.
- **Casual get-togethers or informal parties:** Depending on your timeline, invitations can be presented just prior to the party (make a phone call for a same day or next-day event), up to three weeks in advance.

Chips and Tips

For milestone events such as bar/bat mitzvahs, weddings, or anniversaries, send a save-this-date postcard to out-of-town guests once you have settled on a date to give them sufficient time to make travel or vacation plans.

Aside from sending written invitations, you can use other ways to get the word out about your next party. Some ideas are more suited for your party's style than others, so take care in selecting the appropriate method.

By Word of Mouth

You and your friends are sitting around the office having lunch, trying to figure out what to do for the weekend. Suddenly you say, "Hey, why doesn't everyone come to my place after work on Friday? Bring your swimsuit. We can order in some pizzas." This is an impromptu invitation meant for those within earshot.

Ma Bell Invites

If the event is no more complicated than asking your best friend over for a Sunday barbecue, you can, of course, do it quickly with a phone call.

If you have a lot of phoning to do, you can even start a *phone chain* among several of your guests. Just ask each guest to call one or two other people, and make sure you supply all the names and numbers. It's a great time saver.

Do not rely on phone calls if you have to give detailed information such as directions, special instructions for a surprise party, where to park, or which entrance to use. Remember: When the information is important, write it out and distribute it.

Shindig Sayings

A **phone chain** invitation means that you call one guest and ask him or her to call one or two others whose names and numbers you supply.

Party Pitfall

Never leave a party invitation on an answering machine. You have no way of knowing if the message was ever received. If you must leave an invitation on a recorder, follow up if you have not heard from the guest within a day or two.

Hand Delivery

Are you having a theme party and the guests are all located in close proximity? Or do you want to create a real buzz? Hire costumed couriers (or put your car-driving teens into service) to make the rounds and deliver the invitations by hand. Their outfits should match the party. For instance, if it's a western theme, have the couriers dress as if they worked for the Pony Express.

You've Got Mail

There are now Internet Web sites on which you can quickly extend your invitations via e-mail—in cyber-style. Some even offer programs that will track responses in a guest-list format and provide your own party-plan Web page.

If you know all your guests' e-mail addresses, you can send invitations via e-mail for a high-tech effect. These look like actual cards and can be animated or artsy, formal or fun. All you do is fill in the blanks and in seconds your cyber-invitation will be in their electronic mailboxes.

Best of all, since replying only takes a couple of keystrokes, you generally receive responses much more quickly, which is a big help in your planning. The surprise is that these cyber-summons are FREE! Check out:

- Blue Mountain Arts (www.bluemountainarts.com)
- Evite.com (www.evite.com)
- RSVPme (www.rsvpme.com)
- ersvp (www.ersvp.com)

Party Pitfall

With hand-delivered invitations, discretely call ahead to see if they will be at home or at their place of work (if you can deliver it there). It would be a shame to waste the fun and festivity of such a surprise on an unanswered door.

Printer Party Goods

Use your desktop publishing or clip-art programs to help you design and print an invitation, a matching reply card, program, envelopes, and place card that are one-of-a-kind and totally customized for your event.

Whichever invitation you choose, make sure it matches the theme of your event. And, most importantly, have fun doing it!

The Least You Need to Know

- The invitation is your guests' first glimpse into your party; let it be crystal clear.
- Match your invitation to your party style: casual for casual, formal for formal.
- All invitations must answer the five *W*s: who, what, when, where, why—sometimes how.
- There are limited occasions when word of mouth or telephone invitations are sufficient.
- You can design and send a variety of invitations.

Chapter 9

Tiny Bubbles: Stocking Your Bar

In This Chapter

- Learning the basics of serving alcoholic beverages
- Stocking your bar
- Essential garnishes to have on hand
- Buying just the right glassware

When your palate (and the occasion) calls for something a little more sophisticated than a six pack of beer or wine that comes in the gallon bottle with the screw-off cap, it's time to start setting up your own home bar.

A walk around a liquor store will reveal everything from wines to whiskey, from liquors to liqueurs, from apple jack to apple cider. Here's everything you need to know to set up a serviceable bar that should be able to handle most basic drinks.

Top Shelf

If you've ever bought a drink in a bar, you probably know that bar-brand liquors are one price and top shelf is a higher price. *Top-shelf* liquors are called that because they are literally kept on the top shelf—right in the eyeshot of the customer.

Top shelf, or *call brands,* are those brand names people ask for: "Give me a Chivas on the rocks."

The bar brands are usually used if you don't specify a certain brand, for drink specials, and as happy-hour promotions. These brands are less expensive and lower in quality than top-shelf brands.

Shindig Sayings

A **top shelf** or **call brand** liquor is more expensive than a bar brand and usually asked for by brand name.

Shindig Sayings

A **boilermaker** is made by dropping a shot glass of bourbon into a mug of beer and immediately gulping it down.

While it's possible to find generic brands that might be the same quality as a top-shelf liquor, you would do better to invest the extra dollar or two in a premium bottle for your home bar. Just as a chef uses only the best ingredients, a good bartender looks for the highest-quality liquors.

Booze Basics

Chances are you have a liquor of choice, but to set up a bar that will appeal to all your guests, here is some information you'll need to be the best barkeeper in town.

Give Me a Whiskey ... Straight

Whiskey actually comes in three basic varieties. There's blended, bourbon, and Scotch.

Blended whiskey is made with a combination of grain and 20–40 malt whiskeys mixed together. It's also the main component in classic cocktails like a Seven and Seven (Seagrams 7 Crown and 7-Up), a manhattan, or an old-fashioned. Want a good whiskey for mixing with colas or clear soda? Choose Seagrams. For drinking straight up or on the rocks, try Dewars.

Bourbon combines at least 51 percent corn with rye, barley, and/or wheat. Bourbon is thought of as the quintessential American whiskey and the classic whiskey chaser in a *boilermaker*.

Festive Facts

When people ask for a bourbon drink made with Jim or Jack, they are referring to Jim Beam or Jack Daniels. Although Jack Daniels is a Tennessee sour mash, most folks drink it as they would a classic Kentucky bourbon.

Scotch, thought by many people to be the Cadillac of the whiskeys, is usually served straight or on the rocks (over ice). It's occasionally mixed with water or club soda, but for the most part people who favor it like the taste of the Scotch itself. If you really want to make people blanch, ask for a Scotch and 7-Up. Chivas Regal is the premiere brand, and Dewars also makes a very good Scotch.

If you are looking for a good Scotch, look for a single-malt made by one brewery and imported from Scotland.

In addition to the more common whiskies, there is also Canadian whisky (spelled without the e), Irish whiskey, and rye whiskey.

The Lighter Drinks

For folks who like to drink light, most choose a clear gin or vodka. A gin and tonic is still the classic summer drink—kind of like tart lemonade with a kick. Some folks also use gin to make martinis, although over the years vodka has become more synonymous with that drink. Gin mixes well with a variety of fruit juices, and Tanqueray or Beefeaters are good brands to buy.

Chips and Tips

Many bartenders recommend that if you want to buy only one bottle of alcohol, it should be vodka since it is so versatile.

Vodka is the main ingredient in martinis and is made from grain. Although there are flavored vodkas, keep a plain bottle of Stolichnaya (known more commonly as Stoli) or Absolut chilled in your fridge or freezer to be drunk straight. Vodka also mixes well with a variety of juices.

Rums come in both dark and light. The lighter varieties are used as the base for a number of tropical drinks including rum runners, piña coladas, or Long Island iced teas. The darker varieties, while used in some mixed drinks, are often drunk like a whiskey.

Shindig Sayings

A **shooter** is usually made in a shot glass. The recipient drinks the liquor in one gulp, sometimes followed by sucking on a wedge of lime or lemon.

Tequila is an essential in most bars and is usually used as a *shooter*—a shot glass of liquor, served straight and swallowed in one gulp—or mixed into a margarita. Be sure you have coarse salt and lime juice on hand to make a classic margarita. Cuervo Gold is an excellent choice of tequila.

Dry vermouth is needed for gibsons and martinis, while sweet vermouth is needed for Manhattans.

The Wine Cellar

It is also a good idea to have several bottles of wine on hand in your liquor cabinet. You should buy a bottle or two of a merlot or a cabernet for red-wine drinkers. Chardonnay and Chablis should satisfy your white-wine drinkers. If you are not sure which to buy or have a limited budget, split the difference and buy a rosé or white zinfandel.

These days, you can usually buy good inexpensive wines at any wine store. Just ask the clerk if you need help choosing a good wine.

A bottle or two of champagne or sparkling wine kept chilled for special occasions is always nice to have on hand.

Shindig Sayings

Liqueurs are a variety of sweet alcoholic beverages usually made from fruits, nuts, spices, flowers, or essential oils. Although they were traditionally served after dinner to aid digestion, today they are also used in the preparation of a variety of cocktails and cooking recipes.

After-Dinner Drinks

Liqueurs are generally served after dinner or with dessert. Made from fruits, nuts, spices, and flowers, liqueurs traditionally have been served to aid in digestion and cleanse the palate after a large meal. While these are nice to have on hand, they are not essential to a basic bar.

Aperitifs are often used synonymously with liqueurs, but are actually different. They are usually sipped before a meal to help whet the appetite. Again, these can be stocked in a more advanced bar.

For the more sophisticated palates, there are a variety of brandies, cognacs, schnapps, ports, and cordials. These, too, can be added to your bar over time.

Nonalcoholic Essentials

Having a wide selection of drink mixers available to your guests will not only help you stretch your liquor further, it also will offer your friends an alternative to alcohol.

In addition to mixes, a well-stocked bar also would have garnishes such as large green olives (without the pimento); orange, lemon, and lime wedges and peels; maraschino cherries; coarse salt; sugar; and pearl onions.

By having all these basics in your bar, you can pretty much guarantee that no one is going to go thirsty at your party.

Taking Stock of Your Liquor Cabinet

No one expects you to have every drink available at his or her favorite cocktail lounge, but there are some basic types that you'll want to buy and then add to your stock over time.

Booze Essentials

You don't have to bust the bank to set up a basic bar. You can buy a bottle at a time until you build up your stock. Ultimately, you should shoot for the basics listed here.

You will always need the following liquors on hand: blended whiskey, bourbon, gin, rye, Scotch, tequila, and vodka.

Since you can't always stock your bar with a collection of wines, unless you happen to be Donald Trump, try this to get yourself started: Rosé or white zinfandel, light white wine like chablis or chardonnay, and a red wine such as a merlot or burgundy.

Beer is one of the most popular party beverages and can be found in hundreds of styles and alcoholic and nonalcoholic varieties.

Every good party host has a collection of mixers, or beverages commonly mixed with liquor. With the mixers mentioned here you will be able to make almost any drink your guests request. They include club soda, colas, fruit juices, ginger ale, milk or cream, tonic water, and coffee.

And, of course, never forget the ice. Running out of ice can be a party breaker, so make sure that when you buy your liquor you stock up on bags of ice.

Chips and Tips

To salt or sugar a glass, rub the rim first with a wedge of citrus fruit (orange juice for sugar, lemon or lime for salt). Pour some coarse salt or sugar into a small saucer. Invert the glass into the dish and twist. The glass's rim will be coated.

Supplementing Your Stock

If you find that you have more money and can afford more expensive liquors, you might want to consider adding liqueurs, brandies, aperitifs, rum, and vermouth to your liquor cabinet. They will expand on the variety of drinks you'll be able to offer your guests. Keep track of your friends' favorite drinks to lead you to buy the best choices.

Chips and Tips

Juices mixed with sparkling water make a great nonalcoholic beverage for any guest who doesn't want to imbibe.

Again, mixers are essential to every party, and the more variety you have the happier your guests will be. As you increase your stock, consider purchasing Bloody Mary mix, daiquiri mix, grenadine, simple syrup, Tabasco sauce, and Worcestershire sauce.

Garnishes are the treats often served with a mixed drink. It is good to have at least some of the following on hand. Put in a stock of celery sticks, lemons, limes, maraschino cherries, unstuffed green olives, pearl onions, oranges, course salt, and granulated sugar.

As your bartending mastery grows, these drink-enhancing garnishes are sure to please and astonish your guests: angostura bitters, cinnamon sticks, cloves, nutmeg, powdered chocolate, paper umbrellas, and whipped cream. Check your drink recipes before your party to lay in a stock of what you'll need.

Winning Ways with Wine

For a cocktail party, it's good to have one or more bottles of a red, white, and rosé or white zinfandel wine on hand. For a dinner party, choose the wine that best goes with your meal and buy a sufficient quantity to pour two glasses per guest in the first hour, one glass per guest for each subsequent hour.

Red wine is generally served with heavy dishes such as beef or pasta. White wines help accent fish, pork, poultry, and salads. Rosé and white zinfandels are gaining in popularity as all-purpose wines but should not be used if there are wine connoisseurs present.

For those occasions in life that call for corks to pop, keep a bottle of champagne or a sparkling wine in your refrigerator at all times. You can't always predict those celebratory moments.

Party Pitfall

Beer should be poured and served in glasses. The bottle or can should never leave the bar area. There is nothing more likely to ruin photographs at a formal event than pictures of your guests holding bottles or cans of beer.

Beer Barrel Polka

While it's always nice to stock the favorite beer brand of your guests, a party is a good time to experiment with new flavors and brands. Purchase a six-pack or two of an imported beer or a local microbrew. If it is a sports-related event or for a big gang, you will probably want to tap a small keg and keep the beer free-flowing.

For the beer baron, you might want to consider stocking different varieties of beer. There are ales, stouts, lagers, pilsners, and more. The list is endless. Be sure to stock nonalcoholic varieties as well.

Tool Time

Just as a chef needs the right tools to cook, a bartender needs the right equipment to be a good mix master.

A corkscrew is essential for opening wine bottles. If you are not used to working with one, you would be wise to buy a wing corkscrew. They are easy to operate and make extracting the cork simpler for beginning wine stewards.

If you want to make the perfect martini, you will need a shaker. It's a container, usually made of stainless steel or glass, that looks like an oversized tumbler. A shaker often comes with a stirrer and a strainer. The strainer is essential for keeping ice cubes or fruit slices from falling into the serving glass.

To measure the right amount of alcohol in drink recipes, you will need a jigger. In a pinch, you also can use a shot glass.

Don't be fooled by your bar guide. When a recipe calls for a teaspoon, it is not referring to the spoon you use to stir your tea. Head to your nearest kitchen gadget store to pick up a real set of measuring spoons.

A "church key" can and bottle opener are still useful items, even with today's flip-top cans and screw-cap bottles. Many microbrews or imports don't use screw caps and you'll have to rely on old-fashioned bottle openers.

Swizzle sticks or straws (short and tall) are good to put into mixed drinks for stirring and sipping.

A pitcher with a long-handled spoon to mix and serve drinks is good to have for iced tea, lemonade, or a large batch of a frozen drink.

A wine bucket is nice to have to properly chill the champagne, but a good-looking ice bucket and tongs are essential.

Every good mixologist has several bar towels by his side for cleanups and wiping water spots off glasses.

Chips and Tips

If you don't know your pony from your jigger, this conversion table should help you create your cocktail concoction.

1 dash = ⅙ teaspoon

1 teaspoon = ⅛ ounce

1 tablespoon = 3 teaspoons

1 pony = 1 ounce

1 jigger = 1¼ ounces

1 red wine glass = 4 ounces or ½ cup

1 white wine glass = 6 ounces or ¾ cup

1 cup = 8 ounces

Party Pitfall

Using paper towels instead of linen can leave unsightly lint on your glasses or bar.

Toothpicks are helpful for skewering the cocktail garnish.

A small, sharp paring knife is necessary to cut garnishes and fruit peels.

Bar tools essential for every mixologist.

Make certain you have a supply of cocktail napkins on hand to give out with each drink. In addition to keeping the condensation from making the glasses slippery, it also will help to keep water marks off your furniture. Coasters are essential for fine wood surfaces.

Chips and Tips

When a twist of lemon peel is called for in a drink recipe, with a sharp knife, cut a strip of lemon peel from the fruit and rub around the rim of the glass. Twist the peel over the drink to release the skin's oil and drop the oil and peel into the drink.

Ice Is Nice

Red wine and straight-up drinks are about the only beverages served at room temperature at a cocktail party. Everything else you serve should be chilled.

Beer glasses should be kept chilled to avoid excess foam when the beer is poured. If you don't have room for the glasses in the freezer, swish ice cubes around the inside of the glass and dump the cubes out before pouring the beer. Make sure, however, that you have some glasses that are not chilled for those who feel it takes away from the taste of the beer.

On average, guests go through 2½ pounds of ice per person during a standard four-hour party, and more so in hot weather. Remember, you can never have too much ice. If you can't make enough, buy it. Keep it in coolers and use it to replenish your ice buckets. The bags of ice are not meant to be seen by your guests. Be discreet when you restock. For sanitary purposes, ice should be picked up with tongs, not your fingers.

Remember that you'll need more ice for frozen drinks.

Party Pitfall

Standard-sized ice cubes can damage blender motors and dull or break blades, so make sure to use an ice crusher before dropping ice into the blender when mixing your frozen drink.

Class with Glass

We know you loved collecting them, but when you're hosting a cocktail party, you probably should serve your guests' drinks in something other than your Flintstone jelly glasses or the matching Sesame Street cups from McDonald's. Relax, you can still use them at a theme party.

Besides your theme glasses, there are a few essential glasses you should have, or at least know about, when throwing a party.

Basic bar glassware.

A highball glass is a good, versatile glass. It will hold between 8 and 12 ounces of fluid. It can be used for a Tom Collins, iced tea, Bloody Mary, or a similar tall drink.

An old-fashioned or on-the-rocks glass is short and fat and will hold approximately 6–8 ounces. As its name implies, you can serve an old-fashioned or shots of liquor poured on the rocks. In daily use, it serves as a generous juice glass.

Chips and Tips

Always handle a glass by its stem when preparing a drink. You don't want your fingerprints to dirty the glass or the heat of your hand to warm the chilled surface.

If you can only afford to buy just one type of wine glass, go with a larger stemmed red wine glass. The bowl shape will hold 8–10 ounces. This will also work well as a water glass. When your budget allows, purchase smaller matching white wine glasses that will hold 6–8 ounces.

In a pinch, you can use a wine glass to serve champagne. However, to help trap the champagne's bubbles and retain its sparkling flavor, you should invest in 6-ounce flute glasses.

Chips and Tips

To avoid wasting beverages, and glasses, personalize plastic beverage glasses with guests' names. If you prefer glass, buy labels to put on the glasses and then add your guest's name with waterproof ink.

To help make mixed drinks, find a 2-ounce shot glass. It's preferable to find one that's already marked for a 1-ounce shot.

As your bartending skills grow, there are some other glass styles you might want to add to your collection.

For the ultimate in savoir-faire, wrap your hands around a 12- to 20-ounce snifter and let the warmth of your hands heat your favorite after-dinner brandy.

Nothing looks quite the same as a classic 8-ounce martini glass. Here's lookin' at you, kid.

And for the ladies who lunch or for the trendy folks who prefer flavored vodka, there's the chic style of a 2-ounce cordial glass.

Another staple of sophisticated society is the 5- to 7-ounce sherry glass used to serve aperitifs or liqueurs.

Want to add some kick to your coffee? Pour your best brew into an 8- to 10-ounce Irish coffee mug along with a shot of Irish whiskey. Top with whipped cream and you'll have a drink that ballads have been written about. These mugs also can be used for layered drinks.

Festive Facts

Greta Garbo, the legendary film actress, spoke her first American film words in the 1930 MGM version of *Anna Christie.* "Give me a whiskey, ginger ale on the side—and don't be stingy, baby." Dubbed the "Swedish Sphinx," she retired from films in 1941 and remained almost a recluse until her death in 1990.

Be Responsible

Finally, remember that if you're the one pouring the drinks or hosting the party, you are responsible for your guests. Even if you were not legally at risk, you are morally accountable to stop friends from driving while intoxicated or even marginally under the influence.

Set up a designated driver, take their car keys away from them, call a cab, or put them up for the night. The bottom line is, don't let friends drive drunk. If you do, you're not a good friend.

The Least You Need to Know

- Buy the best brand of liquor you can afford.
- You can stock a basic bar and build on it over time.
- Invest in the right mixing equipment.
- When you're starting out, buy glasses that can be used for a variety of beverages.
- Be responsible—don't let your guests drink and drive.

Chapter 10

Setting Up Your Space

In This Chapter

- Pre-party cleaning
- Preparing the powder room
- Finding parking for everyone
- Party safety tips

The home you so carefully decorated and made into a snug sanctuary might not be a haven to the hoards of guests you've invited to your party. You undoubtedly designed it to suit your own day-to-day life—but that isn't necessarily conducive to company.

In fact, throwing a party at home might mean that you need to spend some time rearranging furniture, removing pictures, and even putting things in storage. In this chapter, you'll learn about just some of the things you can do to make your home into more of a party space.

The Party Is Here

Once you've decided on the type of party and the amount of guests, look around your home and decide where you want the group to gather.

If you've informally entertained before, where did your company congregate? Often during casual events, people tend to naturally assemble in one area of your home

Chips and Tips

If you prefer to keep your cooking area hidden while you're preparing for a party and you have an open design with a counter that allows anyone to look in, make or buy a screen for privacy. Place the screen on the countertop to keep the kitchen hidden from view.

more than others. If that's the case, will this room be suitable for a planned celebration? What is it about that room that makes it attractive for guests to gather? Can you duplicate that feeling in another room if you need to hold the party there?

Don't look at a room and assume it has only one purpose. While dining rooms might seem the most logical setting for a dinner party, a kitchen, den, or living room might work if they can accommodate more guests. In fact, many hosts say that whenever people are invited to their home, no matter where the party is planned to take place, everyone ends up in the kitchen.

Working with Your House's Layout

Many modern homes have an open floor plan that allows for a free flow of guests. If your layout is like that, it often makes an ideal setup for large-scale entertaining. Just be sure to incorporate all the adjoining areas into your party plan. For instance, you might be able to set up the food in one area, the bar in another, and the entertainment in still another. This way guests will take advantage of all the available space.

In older homes where there is a designated living room, dining room, kitchen, family room, basement, or den, choose the space that will best accommodate the number of guests and the activities planned, and has easy access.

Don't rule out any room or space for a party without careful consideration, even if the area doesn't initially seem primed to hold party-goers.

Additional Party Spaces

For some folks, the garage or unfinished basement is a great place to gather—especially when crafts or kids are involved. It's often an area that can take friends dropping food or paint being splattered. Just remove the car, do some quick cleanups, add some decorations, and these areas become Party Central.

Will the weather conditions cooperate? Then don't forget the great outdoors. Backyards, patios, terraces, and decks can be the site of a variety of celebrations, not just barbecues.

Once you've settled on a space, evaluate if you can make it more user-friendly.

Sit on It

Is your living room or den set up with the chairs facing the television set as the focal point? Unless part of the entertainment involves sitting and watching a program or video, change your seating. Arrange your chairs together in conversation groupings so guests can talk easily, even if it puts their backs to the television.

However, don't put the furniture so close together that people can't easily walk around. Most folks only need about 18 inches to comfortably move between pieces of furniture. Also, make sure that a table or flat surface is within easy reach of a seated guest for placing a cup or plate.

Unless it's a small group or sit-down dinner party, or you want your guests to stay fixed in their chairs like potted plants, provide seating for no more than one quarter to one half of your guests, depending on the age group.

If people seem glued to their seats when you want them to mingle, the amount of seating might not be the problem. It's possible that it's the wrong type of seating. Big, cushy couches aren't necessarily convenient when you need to get up and down at a cocktail party. You might do better to put in three dining room chairs and take out a loveseat. That not only gives you an extra seat, it also makes the arrangement more portable.

Party Pitfall

Don't plan to hold your event outdoors unless you know for certain the weather will be pleasant or you have arranged for a tent or other shelter should the conditions turn from fair to foul.

Party Pitfall

If your party list is filled with the elderly or infirm, do reserve adequate seating for all your guests.

It Looks Better Over There

If there is too much furniture in the room you plan to have your party in, move some of the pieces out. You might be able to use them in another area or store them elsewhere like a bedroom, basement or garage. You also might consider moving the pieces outside in good weather or taking them over to the house of a neighbor or friend.

When you have a lot of furniture to remove and not enough places to store it, consider renting a moving truck for the day to hold some of your belongings.

Too Massive to Move

You will find you have pieces of furniture that are simply too big to budge. If that's the case and it just looks out of place with your party decor, there are a few things you can do.

One way is through camouflage—covering a hutch with fish nets for a nautical party, for instance.

Chips and Tips

If you need to hire laborers to help with moving furniture, call a local college job board or look in your Yellow Pages under "Employment, Temporary." There are a number of agencies that specialize in manual laborers that can be hired for four hours or more.

You can also turn the seating away from those specific home furnishings. Move guests' focus to another object or objects.

Hiding the Heirlooms

If you have a favorite vase or a priceless painting put those precious pieces away for safekeeping. Of course you can show them off, but do it in either smaller groups or set up barriers around the piece.

Cleaning and Clutter

If your home could be described as having a lived-in look, you might want to do some basic housekeeping before your party.

Cleaning Away Clutter

It's difficult to clean around a stack of magazines, a pile of shoes, a week's worth of mail, arts and crafts projects, and general jumble. For the best results, before a cleaning product touches your hand, you must first clear the clutter.

Chips and Tips

If you can, plan your parties to take place shortly after you've done your major spring or fall cleaning. This way your home looks its best, and your party preparations will involve little more than dusting, vacuuming, and washing the floors.

Use Suitable Supplies

Once the clutter has been dealt with, it's time to start cleaning. To save time, purchase or make a cleaning belt similar to one a carpenter uses to keep nails, screws, and tools. A pair of cargo pants with multiple pockets also will work, as will a bucket or tray with a handle that is filled with cleaning equipment. Try to limit your cleaning products to a few choices. Use multipurpose products for greater speed and efficiency.

Clean Smarter, Not Harder

When you begin to clean, use the clock system. When you enter a room, clean it as if you were going around a clock and you have started at 12 o'clock. Move from there to 1, then 2, and so on, until you've worked your way around the clock and are back at 12. Don't backtrack. Dirt follows gravity and floats down, so dust the ceiling fans and light fixtures before you vacuum the floors.

Get all suitable members of the household involved in the cleaning. If they worked hard to make it spotless, they're less likely to want to see it get dirty again.

Remember, you're going for the "illusion" of clean. It's a party, not a military inspection of your barracks.

Chips and Tips

Black-and-white newspapers make excellent, lint-free cleaning cloths for windows and mirrors.

Off Limits

As much as you'd like to have guests feel completely comfortable in your home, chances are there will be some areas that you will like to keep off limits. You have every right to keep guests out of certain areas, and there are a couple of things you can do short of posting a guard.

The simplest way to suggest that a room is off-limits is to close the room's door. That will generally keep most mature guests at bay.

However, if you're having a party with lots of children in attendance and you truly want to keep the kids out of certain rooms, you might want to replace your doorknobs with ones that have simple locks or install a simple hook-and-eye lock near the top of the door out of a child's reach.

Party Pitfall

A computer can be very tempting to nosy guests. To keep them off, install a password or a key lock so no one can turn on your computer without your permission. It also might be advisable to simply unplug it and cover it with plastic.

Preparing the Powder Room

The one room in the house you will want to make sure is spotless is your powder room. Provide a box of tissues on the counter and store an extra roll of toilet tissue under the sink or in a special reserve container.

Surveys say that most guests will snoop in a friend's medicine cabinet. Remove all medicines that could potentially cause problems if taken incorrectly and move them to a locked area.

If there are not going to be small children at your event, you might want to put together a toiletries basket for your powder room with likely items your guests will need.

Festive Facts

Even when you are not entertaining, a bathroom's medicine chest is not the ideal storage area for drugs. The warm, moist atmosphere can break down or change the chemical composition of some prescriptions. All drugs—prescription or over the counter—should routinely be kept in a cool, dry place.

The Comforts of Home

With a little effort, your guests can enjoy all the comforts of their home—in your home.

When the weather is raining or cold and guests will be wearing outer garments, try to arrange for closet space or another area where these coats and jackets can be hung. While many people routinely place coats on a bed, it makes it very inconvenient if your coat is on the bottom of the pile and you want to leave early. A sturdy clothesline, hung in your garage or spare room, will serve as a rack for coats on heavy-duty hangers.

In addition to providing coat racks, you should also be aware of temperature. Your guests' comfort might depend on your heat and air-conditioning system. Adjust your thermostat accordingly.

Chips and Tips

Place an attractive can of air freshener within sight so that guests can use it at their own discretion.

Chips and Tips

Place a "Do Not Touch" sign over the thermostat to ward off a well-meaning guest who wants to change the room's climate.

The Thoughtful Host

If you know that a friend has difficulty walking, place his or her chair at the end of a table and near the exit (and bathroom) to make moving about easier. Also, reserve a parking spot close to your house or in your driveway.

Speak with guests who may need special attention in advance to see if there are small changes you can easily accomplish in your home to make him or her feel as welcome and comfortable as any other guest.

Besides taking your guests into consideration, it is also important to consider how a party might affect those who live near you. If your neighbors live close by and it's possible your party will inconvenience them in some way, alert them to your plans. Better still, if it's a large party, invite them. Even if they choose not to attend, they are less likely to complain or feel put out if they know you have been considerate.

Park It There

Often one of the major challenges in home entertaining is providing enough parking spaces. If this will be a problem at your party, try these solutions:

- Move your own car out of your driveway or parking slot and tell a guest or two they can have your spot.
- Check with neighbors to see about using their parking spots or driveways.
- Suggest that friends park in a nearby parking lot and arrange for at least two cars to shuttle your guests back and forth.

When parking is truly inconvenient or extremely limited, you might consider hiring a valet service. This is especially true if your guests are older, would have difficulty walking a great distance, or during bad weather.

Better Safe Than Sorry

The majority of accidents happen around the home. Try to ensure they don't happen at your home during your party. Even if you don't have children of your own, you should try to make your space as safe as possible for your young guests. Use common sense and don't expect that parents will be responsible for their child's actions. In the excitement of a party, too often parents become distracted.

Take a walk through your home at the same time of day that your party will take place and check for safety points like proper lighting, steps in good repair, floor coverings are fastened, and doorways clear of "traffic-jam" items. Also be sure all pets are secure or boarded elsewhere to prevent mishaps. This little exercise can save you a lot of concern and will prevent any party problems.

Keep in mind that if you have something in your home that will make you say "Watch out" or "Don't touch" whenever anyone goes near it, it is best to remove it or secure it before your guests arrive.

Party Pitfall

Whenever there will be open flames, keep a fire extinguisher within reach. They are more efficient than other methods of fire control.

The Least You Need to Know

- Rearrange, move, or camouflage your furniture as needed to make your home party perfect.
- Clear out the clutter before you clean up.
- Prep a pretty powder room.
- Notify the neighbors of your party.
- Make parking plans to accommodate all guests.

Chapter 11

Ambience: Beyond Balloons and Crepe Paper

In This Chapter

- Using your senses to create a party atmosphere
- Finding the perfect music for your theme
- Creating party ambience
- Making your buffet table a sensory success

Ambience is that indefinable something—the mood or feeling you get when you walk into a room. It's what makes you feel excited, scared, happy, relaxed, nervous, nostalgic, or sad without even necessarily knowing why.

In this chapter, you'll learn how to produce the right ambience by utilizing four of your five senses: sound, smell, touch, and sight. It is in weaving these elements so skillfully together that you are not totally aware of them separately that you create ambience. They just come together to create an atmosphere that affects you on an almost subconscious level. It's knowing how to utilize sound, songs, fabrics, flowers, props, and lighting.

Now Hear This

How often have you heard a song or a sound and been reminded of a different time and place? Sound is a very strong stimulus. Close your eyes and think about the beach. In addition to the water, sun, and sand, you're probably also thinking about the calls of gulls flying overhead, music playing from a radio, children laughing, and waves crashing onto the shore. Sound goes a long way to creating ambience.

Party Pitfall

Be sure to give your DJ a clear picture of your guests, theme, and occasion. You'd hate for a disc jockey to show up stocked with popular dance and disco music if your guests are all in their late 60s and 70s.

At your party, sounds could be anything from piano music to creaking doors and crying ghouls as part of a haunted house theme. Specially created sound-effect tapes and CDs, along with music, are effective ways to add an aural dimension to all your parties.

Keep in mind when planning your party that it is important to select sounds and music that are appropriate to the event or location. For instance, it's unlikely a Sweet 16 party would feature the music of Mozart. On the other hand, rock and roll wouldn't be fitting for a high tea. Music, like other sounds, should be appropriate to the site, the occasion, and the crowd.

Choose the right sounds at a theme party and you have created another dimension that will make your parties stand out from any party your guests have ever been to.

Festive Facts

Draped with trees and vines from floor to ceiling, the Rainforest Cafe, a national chain of jungle-themed restaurants, recreates all the visual elements of a rainforest. However, the designers went a step farther and included the aural atmospheric elements of animatronic animals, waterfalls, squawking parrots and macaws, and the sounds of a thunderstorm. The entire experience of dining is enhanced tremendously by the sounds you hear.

Sweet Smell of Success

Smell is one of the most effective senses to help remind you of a time or place in your past. While it's fun to use fragrances to enhance a party's theme, use scents sparingly and carefully. It is far better to have your guests tempted by the smell of steak sizzling on your grill than it is to have the heady fragrance of the stargazer lily in your centerpiece or scented candles. Strong scents can distort the taste of your dinner.

How Touching

If you think about why you love a favorite outfit, you'll probably realize that part of what you like is how the clothes feel next to your skin, their softness, and maybe their coziness. The elements of touch you select to create ambience for your party should also feel good next to your guests' skin.

Fabrics are a terrific way to stimulate the sense of touch. When decorating, you can use rich patterned tapestry wall hangings, downy-soft seat cushions, satin throws, the rustic texture of burlap tablecloths, the luxurious feel of velvet pillows, or the absorbency of cotton napkins. All of these fabrics can be a great way to capture guests' attention as well as sustaining the party's theme.

If you want to give your home the illusion of being a medieval castle, drape your chairs in tapestry. However, if you want to give guests the feel of being in the home of a peasant in the same time period, remove any soft cushions. Instead, give guests wooden seats or cover your chairs in burlap to make them scratchy.

Chips and Tips

Be sure the scents you surround your guests with don't interfere with the fragrance of your feast. The wrong or too strong fragrance can ruin their appetites.

Party Pitfall

During a lecture event or anything that could be considered slightly dull, make sure the temperature is a little colder than normal and the chairs comfortable, but not overly so. You don't want your guests to be lulled to sleep by a comfy chair and a warm room.

A Soft Seat

The sense of touch has just as much to do with your guests' comfort level as anything else.

When providing seating for your guests, it is very important to consider what kind of party you are having. At a cocktail or networking party remove cushy couches and put out chairs that are more along the lines of a church pew—in other words, not exactly a place you would plant yourself for the entire evening.

However, if you have arranged for stage entertainment or a floor show, make the seating fairly comfortable.

A Touchy Theme

Just like music, what your guests touch at your party should vary from theme to theme. If the party has a Japanese theme, you expect to sit on pillows on the floor and cool yourself with paper fans. At a garden party, you might find a hammock or porch swing more appropriate.

When you choose the items you'll need to convey your theme, consider not only what the materials or props will look like, but what they will feel like. For instance, do you want your guests to feel as if they have stepped into a sensuous Arabian nights fantasy with silk and satin cushions and table coverings? Or are they to feel as if they are experiencing the rustic retreat of the Wild West with wicker baskets, rough-hewn cedar tables, and well-oiled leather chairs?

Luminous Lighting

The bright light you use to cook and clean in your kitchen is probably a little harsher than the light you have in your bedroom and living room. In most other rooms of the house, your lighting is softer because you don't need that same bright intensity as you do when you are chopping vegetables.

Chips and Tips

Check out your room at the same time of day as your party is scheduled to be held. Turn lights on and off, change bulb wattage, move lamps, light candles—experiment. Have someone sit in different parts of the room so you can see how the lighting makes your guests look.

To create the best lighting scheme, illuminate from above, below, and from the sides of the room, all at the same time. Use low wattage, soft white, pink, or frosted bulbs. Install dimmers for the greatest range of lighting effects.

There's a saying: "If all the world's a stage, then I want better lighting." Be sure your parties and your guests are seen in their best light.

Candlelight

For an overall flattering effect, you can't beat candlelight or a fireplace. If you want to create an instantly romantic or dramatic effect, eliminate every other light source and fill your room with candles. The flickering glow is an extremely effective way to illuminate a room and create a warm ambience.

Chips and Tips

To help candles stay drip-free, store them in your refrigerator until a half an hour before you use them. When it's time to light them, keep the candles out of any drafts.

Twinkle, Twinkle

The one Christmas tree decoration you should never pack away are the white twinkle lights. These strands of mini-lights are a powerful light resource. It's not that they illuminate so well—it's just that the effect they give is so dramatic.

String them in trees, line a walkway, outline a piece of furniture or a doorway, tuck them into bushes, weave them into a centerpiece, drape them on a curtain rod, wrap around poles, or let them shine through sheer fabric. Place these twinkle lights in almost any area you can think of, for almost every occasion. Twinkle lights are a great resource for creating interesting lighting effects.

Illuminating Luminarias

Often at Christmas you will see streets decorated with paper bags filled with glowing tea lights or votive candles. It's an impressive sight when you see them lining walkways, driveways, and the curbs in front of homes.

While you can buy premade luminarias, you can make them yourself for pennies. All you need is small plain paper bags, a hole punch, kitty litter or sand, and tea lights or votives.

In the top half of a paper bag, use a stencil or freeform a design. Cut out the design with a hand-held punch. Fill a bag halfway with sand or kitty litter. Nestle a votive candle or tea light in the sand, light, and enjoy.

You Light Up My Life

One of the most interesting lighting effects you can use in your home, whether you are planning a party or not, is to set an *uplight* on the floor, underneath a tree or plant.

As the light shines up through the leaves, it will cast beautiful shadows and designs on your ceiling and upper walls.

Chips and Tips

Tuck the strands of twinkle lights in your trees and plants in your home year-round, whether you are preparing for a party or not. They add an unexpected touch of whimsy like fireflies when flashing or elegance when in a nonflashing mode.

Party Pitfall

Don't emboss the pattern all the way through the luminaria bag's length, or the sand or kitty litter will seep out.

Center of Attention

If you're short on money or time, the place to spend your decorating dollars would be on your centerpiece and buffet design. Since your buffet table is one of the focal points at any party, get more flash for your cash by focusing on your centerpiece and creative food containers.

With exciting and theme-related centerpieces, you can often forgo some of the more extravagant decorating ideas.

Shindig Sayings

Uplights resemble a wide tube or a can with the light bulb inserted at the bottom so that it can shine up.

Clothing the Table

Of course, paper and plastic tablecloths and napkins are less expensive than cloth, and they come in a wide variety of colors and patterns, but whenever possible splurge on lavish linens or clever coverings.

You don't need to own a warehouse full of linens to top your tables with style or imagination, nor do you have to break the bank to achieve the look you want. That's one of the advantages to renting. You can choose the size and style that suits your party and purse and you don't even have to press it! If your local store doesn't carry the design you want, have your chosen linens shipped. Panache Party Rentals (www.linenswithpanache.com), for instance, has a huge selection of high-quality rental cloths to choose from that are affordably priced.

Chips and Tips

Always order several additional napkins in case your guests drop theirs and you need to replace them. They also can be used to line baskets or tie to chafing dishes to incorporate your scheme into your overall buffet.

Party Pitfall

Although you can put a square overlay on a round table, on an oblong table, a round overlay doesn't work as well.

Sometimes a tablecloth isn't your only option for topping the table. Perhaps there is a bedsheet in your linen closet that suits your needs, or you can buy fabric on sale often for less than the cost of a tablecloth.

Get creative! Here are some ideas for materials you can use to cover the table for a variety of themes: dropcloths, blueprints, beach towels, flags, or baby blankets. This list is limitless. Look around your home for items that will inspire you to build a better buffet.

Unusual Place Mats

Place mats may be perfect when you have an odd-sized table or you want a layered look on top of your linen. On the other hand, runners are regal or rustic, depending upon the design and fabric.

You have a choice of items that can be used as place mats at theme parties. Here are a few ideas to get you started: diapers, kitchen towels, bandannas, or a large silk leaf.

Looking at Layers

Layering cloths is a lovely way to add multiple colors, patterns, and texture to your table. You can drape the top fabric (called an overlay) loosely, put it on the diagonal if it's a square cloth topping a round one, puddle it on the ground, or gather the top cloth and pin to form a scallop design.

On the Level

Have you ever wondered why buffets in magazines and restaurants look so much more artistic than yours? Levels. Most of us take the time to artfully arrange our food on platters, but then ruin the effect by placing the trays flat on the table. Take overturned pots, boxes, paint cans, books, bricks—anything with height—and loosely cover your arrangement with a tablecloth or coordinating fabric. Bunch the material decoratively and display your dishes at different heights for an eye-catching appeal. Or use cake stands, books or other decorative items that will give your buffet height.

Chips and Tips

You can group your collection together to make the centerpiece, or you can intersperse it with other items. For instance, you might sprinkle coins from your collection around like confetti on the banquet table that has a piggy bank for a centerpiece.

Sensational Centerpieces

Centerpieces are the center of attention on your buffet or dining table. While flowers are the most common centerpiece material, they are not the only choice. Bring out your collectibles, trophies, book collection, toys, hats, candle assortments, fruits, vegetables or even a goldfish bowl. Almost anything, attractively grouped together, will make an inventive centerpiece.

Anything that makes you think of your theme will probably work as the perfect centerpiece. Take a moment to look around your house and see what catches your eye.

Chips and Tips

A child's wading pool is a great place to store iced drinks for a beach-themed party.

Clever Containers

Bowls, while generally used as food containers, are not your only serving choice. Depending on your event, there are a variety of selections that will keep your theme and the party's ambience alive. Some are more suitable for dry food, while others would work for a wet or dry dish. Keep in mind you often can nestle a bowl into a variety of these vessels to camouflage them and make them more suitable for display. Here are some items to spark your own brainstorms. Try hollowed-out fruits or vegetables, hats, baskets, coffee or tea pots, or flower pots for starters. What do you have that would work?

Whether purchased at Tiffany's or the thrift store, the components of your party atmosphere or ambience are a statement of your personality, creativity, and flair for fun. Take the time to explore your surroundings and delve into the depths of treasured or stored possessions.

The Least You Need to Know

- Use your senses to create an ambience.
- Match the music and other sounds to the party and guests.
- Choose textures which will allow guests to get a feel for the effect you are trying to achieve.
- Twinkle lights make a great lighting effect for almost all situations.
- If you're short on money or time, invest in your table decor.

Part 3

The Hostess with the Mostess

•••

To throw a really fantastic party you need to do more than just drop a six-pack of beer and a pizza on the table. You need ambience, the right guests, and that certain something that every good host has—that flare for keeping guests happy and things running smoothly.

Everyone dreams of hosting a party where all the guests get along, all the food tastes great, and everything is perfect. Unfortunately, that is rarely the case. Lucky for you, you have this book and us. We've put together this part for the hostess who wants to be the mostess. You'll learn how to greet guests in style, make them comfortable, and make sure that you have all the right food and drinks to keep the party a party.

Chapter 12

The Hospitable Host

In This Chapter

- Welcoming guests in style
- Getting wallflowers off the wall
- Mingling with your guests
- Handling possible party glitches

The most important—we repeat, *most important*—thing for every host to consider is the comfort and enjoyment of their guests. Nothing short of the red-carpet treatment is acceptable. Each step of the way, in every aspect of the plan, the conscientious host puts herself in the shoes of the guest. In fact, one of your final planning steps is to walk from driveway to doorstep then through the whole event to departure. You will then experience, step by step, the flow of the party through your guests' eyes.

In this chapter, you'll learn how to become the host with the most and give your guests the party of their dreams. From the minute they walk through your door, you're going to want your guests to feel like royalty, and by following these simple tips you'll be able to do just that.

Roll Out the Red Carpet

One of the first steps to creating the ultimate comfort is to send a very clear and concise invitation. Ideally, it will provide every bit of information necessary for your guest to prepare for and attend the event, without a moment's stress or confusion.

Chips and Tips

Even with a map and directions, guests can become lost while in an apartment complex or hallways. The height of hospitality is to place people at strategic points to direct guests. Dress your "living signs" in costumes to match your theme for added appeal.

Party Pitfall

Bad weather will put even the cheeriest guest in a grumpy mood. Provide valet parking or at least umbrella escorts to offer the ultimate accommodation.

In Chapter 8, "The Honour of Your Company ...," you found detailed instructions for creating the perfect party invitation. Those instructions are dedicated to ruling out confusion for guests before arriving. This next section will take you through what a good host should do once guests arrive.

With this, the red carpet leading to your party has rolled out to your guest and he has planted his foot firmly upon it.

Continue the red-carpet treatment by leading your guests to your front door with markers such as balloons, signs, ribbons, or reflective tape. These helpful and welcoming symbols shout out, "We can't wait for you to get here!" Your thoughtfulness and thoroughness will bring guests to the party in a cheerful mood.

One hospitable act leads to another, and with each gesture, your guests feel more and more pampered. They will move along the red carpet to your party portal ready for fun and festivity.

Meetings and Greetings

Have you ever arrived at a party and for the first several minutes stood in discomfort not knowing where to go or what to do? You tried to look confident as you looked around for some clue as to your next move. How special did you feel? Well, your party host made a big boo-boo. When each guest is met cordially and given the impression that the party could not possibly start without him or her, the host has done her job, and very well. Be sure there is always a greeter present for guest arrivals.

Coats, Hats, and Gifts

It is ideal to have a helper take coats, gifts, or potluck items from each guest or direct them on where to place items.

Something to Drink?

The most appreciated welcome is an offer of food and beverage. For crowds in a small area, trays of food and drink being passed is the easiest and fastest way to get refreshments into the hands (and mouths) of guests. Otherwise, place bowls or trays of snacks in several easy-to-reach places.

Placing Names and Naming Places

One of the best ways to make guests at a sizable party feel at ease is to give them an attractive name tag and remove the "What was your name, again?" anxiety. When using name tags, these basic rules apply:

- Prepare the tags ahead if possible.
- Never have guests print their own names.
- Type or print names in large block letters.
- Decorate blank tags with small trinkets to match your theme.
- Some fabrics like silk, velvet, and angora are too delicate for glue. Consider using a clip-on or pin-on tag instead.

Chips and Tips

At large events without a check-in table, welcome guests with name tags alphabetically posted on the front door. Affix name tags to a decorative poster covered in plastic wrap to make it easier to remove them.

Give a newcomer a bit of time to become acclimated to the party, hang her coat up, set down gifts or food, and freshen up, before plunging into the festive fray.

Grab a Seat

A great way to make a guest comfortable at a dinner party is to assign each guest a "reserved" seat or table to sit at. Wandering through a room and feeling clumsy about finding an available seat is one situation most people can do without.

When you have more than one table, use tent cards and jazz them up with ribbons, stickers, trinkets, or fancy lettering. Budget-wise hosts will let their party favors double as seating assignments. Some other innovative party "placers" are ...

- shiny red apples for a teacher's luncheon.
- boxes of Cracker Jacks™ for a baseball banquet.
- neon sunglasses for a beach bash.

Now that you have a place for everyone and everyone in his place, labeled and tabled, you can relax and enjoy your meal, the same as your contented and contained celebrants.

Chips and Tips

For a mixed crowd of friends, family, and business associates, arrange seating by putting compatible guests together. In contrast, let guests seat themselves when they're familiar with each other.

Festive Facts

Name tags should be placed on the right shoulder, so that when shaking hands, it is natural for one's eye to fall on that exact spot, making it easy to casually glance at the guest's name.

Getting the Wallflowers off the Wall

Not every guest at your party will want to plop a lampshade on his head and lead the conga line. Some *wallflowers* won't even want to get into the conga line, so as a gracious host, you must accept that. The ideal party plan includes entertainment and activities that guests can take or leave, as they please.

Shindig Sayings

Wallflowers are people who are so shy they remain on the sidelines at parties and dances resembling wallpaper flowers.

If you want to have any organized activities, keep them short and varied and allow your guests to participate at their own comfort level.

Making introductions and encouraging mingling is high on the host's to-do list. At a large party, it will be necessary to appoint official host's helpers to do party tasks, and leave the hosts free to introduce guests to each other. Make it a special point to know something about your guests so that you might find a common interest and say, "John, Bob is the regional vice president of a software design company. Bob, John is the guy I was telling you about who put together my Web site." Any opening that will make a guest comfortable talking to a stranger is welcomed.

The Most the Host Can Do

There are several do's and don'ts for party hosts. Some might seem obvious, but it is those evident details that often get overlooked. If you take these tips to heart, you will stay at the top of the best-host list:

- Act calm even though you may feel harried and hassled.
- Have fun yourself! Remember, it's a party.

- Set a realistic time for the party to end. You should always leave them wanting more.
- Set up a two-sided buffet line, or spread the buffet around so there are no long lines at large parties.
- Offer to serve elderly guests.
- Keep the thermostat and music at acceptable levels.
- Set your menu to consider the tastes and diets of your guests.
- Provide shady places at an outdoor event and spray your yard to keep insects at bay.

Party Pitfall

An enthusiastic hostess planned a birthday dinner for her husband. Unfortunately, she had so many events planned that dinner was delayed for two hours. The elaborate dinner was interspersed with video shows, toasts, songs, and more toasts. The guest of honor then opened 30 gifts. All this time the guests were pretty much expected to remain seated. When finally set free, the guests took with them a memory of not the delicious meal or the beautiful table decor, but the unbearable length of the party.

Sticky Situations

As perfect as the plan may be, there are always times when a host needs to use her fast fix-it skills. Unexpected and uninvited doesn't just pertain to guests, it also describes party situations. Handle these predicaments quickly and with calm, humor, and grace. It will go a long way to diffuse any uncomfortable dilemmas.

The Least You Need to Know

- The perfect host's first thought is the guests' comfort.
- A gracious welcome is a perfect start to any party.
- Name tags and place cards give guests confidence.
- Getting guests to mingle is easy with some help from the host.

Chapter 13

Smooth Moves

In This Chapter

- Hosting a smooth-running party
- Timing the serving of the food
- Setting up the perfect buffet
- Planning a dessert, taco, or sushi bar

The secret to hosting a successful party is to be an "enjoyee" rather than an employee. It is vital for you to organize your party with this goal in mind. If not, you won't be the only one not enjoying yourself. Your guests will have a tough time relaxing when you, the genial host, are dashing around, fussing over details, and not really landing in one place long enough to visit with guests. Having adequate help is not always the solution to this party panic. You need to know the art of smooth moves.

This chapter will help you because it's a collection of tried, true, and new tips to make sure your party runs like a Swiss watch.

Perfect Planning

How smoothly your party moves along depends greatly on how well you prepared before the first guests arrive. If you have been preparing properly, you should have a notebook full of checklists as well as a written schedule. Make sure all the supplies are in place and all your plans are on schedule. Keep your notebook in a convenient spot so you can check it off lists quickly as the evening progresses.

Don't try to be a superhero. You can't do everything yourself. If you live alone, assign a good friend or relative to serve as honorary cohost, or bring in professionals. By spreading out the hosting duties, no one is ever away from the fun for too long.

Party Pitfall

While cohosts are usually wonderful people, be careful not to bog them down too much with duties. They still expect to be guests and have fun.

Chips and Tips

Make sure you post a master copy of your party schedule on the refrigerator or on a cabinet. That way there are no excuses that someone couldn't find his or her list.

In addition to your master list to avoid forgetting something, put together a list of everything that you are serving and the order in which it's being served. Start with the appetizer and move through dessert. Proper preparation will reduce stress so you can have fun too.

Lay out your plan in time order so that you know if and when you need to take something out to thaw 30 minutes before serving. Not only mark the cooking times, but mark down every detail you have to handle along the way.

If you have several people working with you, be sure everyone has a copy of the master schedule and their duties are marked with their initials and their copy is highlighted in a distinct color in case they misplace their list.

Prep Chef

In good restaurants there is not just one chef, but several who are responsible for helping with the preparations. That means washing, chopping, measuring, slicing—any of the preparations that are essential, but take time away from the cooking itself.

If you've ever watched a TV cooking show, you've probably seen how all the ingredients are measured and kept in cups. Then, as needed, the dish or cup is emptied into the other ingredients. This will speed your preparation time. Use disposable bags and plates for your prep work to cut down on dirty dishes.

Keeping It Clean

To keep things in the kitchen running neatly and smoothly, get in the habit of washing and putting away your dishes as you cook. This will keep the disorder down to a minimum. Keep out a dishpan or pot filled with hot soapy water so utensils and plates can soak. This will speed cleanup.

Meals in Minutes

Whatever needs to be done that can be taken care of before the last minute is a time saver. For instance, put salad dressings in a carafe or place butter in a serving dish. Then all that's left is that they be placed on the table.

If possible, store foods in the container they will be cooked or served in so the only last-minute step is to put it on the stove or on the table as it reads on the schedule.

Avoiding Decorating Dilemmas

You should have all your supplies handy. Make sure you have everything assembled and the scissors, hammers, nails, or tape you'll need so you don't waste time looking for a thumbtack. If possible, pre-set your table the day before.

Picking Up

Keeping the kitchen and party area bussed—that is, clean—goes a long way in having your party run smoothly.

Provide a clean trash can in an area that's in sight of the food, but not too close to it. Keep extra bags in the trash can so as you remove one, you can immediately replace it.

Like a restaurant, keep a tray on hand to help you quickly remove dishes to bring to your kitchen.

Chips and Tips

Assemble all your serving dishes in an easy-to-access area. Label each piece with a small piece of paper naming the particular food that is going into that dish. Also, place the proper serving fork, knife, and/or spoon in the plate to save any last-minute frantic searches.

They're Here and Hungry

Every single aspect of your event has a start, middle, and end, especially food and beverage service. Thirst and Hunger are the most unwelcome party guests. You'll find that people will usually show up at a dinner party famished, so you will want to feed them shortly after they arrive.

Munching Hors d'oeuvres

The first hour of a party, the cocktail and socializing time, is as easy or as complicated as you would like it. Blend elaborate appetizers with some prepare-ahead selections. It will result in less stress during the party.

Party Pitfall

A trash can that is more than half full becomes an unappetizing eyesore. Empty the trash often.

Keep the Drinks Moving

Whether you have hired a bartender or guests are helping themselves, waiting lines are a moving violation. If you have a large group, set up a satellite bar for soft drinks, beer, and wine, making mixed drinks from the main bar only.

The key to timing the cocktail hour is to watch the clock before guests drink or eat too much. Call them to dinner in a graceful way; you can ring a bell, walk and talk while you shepherd guests to the table, or if you have an entertainer with a microphone, have him make the announcement. While you cannot drag them to the table by the scruff of the neck, a gentle nudge will work.

Plated to Perfection

One of the challenges of serving a big dinner is getting all of the food on the table at the same time and at the perfect temperature. Whatever the temperature your food requires, piping hot soup, chilled and crispy salad, hot main course, or frozen dessert, it needs to be served on time.

Self-Serve Situations

Buffet-style service is a boon to events from kickback casual to elegantly formal. There is a basic (and very flexible) set of rules for setting up a socially correct and smoothly operating buffet table.

Chips and Tips

Provide light snacks for guests to enjoy while they wait for their table to be called. A tray with raw vegetables or a basket of bread will work nicely.

Party Pitfall

To avoid running out of popular food items before all guests have passed through the buffet line, have a server mete them out. When everyone has been served once, guests are welcome to visit the buffet for seconds. Or you can serve seconds yourself so no one is embarrassed about looking like they're eating too much.

A basic buffet arrangement should begin at one end of the table picking up plates, then the main dish, vegetables, salads, breads, condiments, and finally flatware and napkins. For greater ease, wrap napkins around flatware.

If seating is available to all guests, then utensils, beverage containers, and napkins are set on the dining table at each place.

For 50 or more guests, your buffet should be available from two sides with identical access to food from either side. Or use a "traffic cop" approach to direct guests to start at both ends and work toward the middle. Set up identical service on both halves.

To accommodate a large number of guests, seat them and call them in turn by table numbers. Try to make sure the waiting line is only slightly longer than the buffet table itself.

Instead of one long table, separate two round tables to be used—one for salads, relishes, and breads, and the second for entrées and vegetables. This encourages guests to make one trip for salads and another for the main course.

If your guests will not be sitting at a table, serve only bite-sized finger/fork/toothpick foods. There should be no need for a knife in these situations.

Grazing

Another trendy form of serving buffet-style is called grazing, since it sends guests roaming from table to table, helping themselves to a variety of foods.

The grazing system requires guests to queue up in several mini lines. This is on-the-move mealtime at its optimum.

A fix-it-yourself grazing station usually features just one meal course such as beverages, salads, bread, sandwiches, soups, entrées, or desserts.

Festive Facts

In 1924 Caesar Cardini invented the Caesar salad at his restaurant in Tijuana, Mexico. He was deluged by a large crowd of Americans on July 4 and it caused him to run out of ingredients. Not one to give up, he hauled what he had out to the dining room and improvised the salad. Cardini's is the label he established in 1948 for the bottled version of his dressing.

Not Just a Salad Bar ...

One of the best innovations that developed from the buffet table was the salad bar. The idea of being able to heap a bed of lettuce, different salad fixings, and your favorite salad dressing onto your plate took the country by storm. There's no limit to what you can put on your salad bar.

There are a variety of theme food bars that will please your guests. These include breakfast bars, appetizer bars, potato bars, *crépe* bars, pasta bars, taco bars, sushi bars, and dessert bars. Almost anything can be put on a grazing bar.

Food bars are a solution to the dilemma of too little space, time, and help. What kind of bar do you want to build?

Shindig Sayings

Crépe is the French word for "pancake." Not to be confused with the thick buttermilk variety Americans eat, these are superthin and with a variety of fillings that make them suitable for appetizer, entrée, or dessert.

Here a Snack, There a Snack

When your space is small and your guests are many, make it simple for them to get food without having to fight their way to the buffet table. Place snack foods within convenient reach and you will be giving your guests a gracious gift ... food on demand.

Place containers of snacks everywhere. With bites and bits just an arm's length away, your guests will be fed throughout the party.

Another way to make food accessible is by passing food on trays. Tidbits on toothpicks and other bite-sized selections work best for this process. Be sure to hand out napkins with each serving. This tactic will reduce the steady stream to the buffet table and the jams it creates, and can be delegated to a helper or volunteer cohost.

Party Pitfall

Avoid getting ambushed by hungry hordes when passing around appetizers. If you find yourself being "attacked" by a throng of people and you can't venture further into the room, place a clean napkin across one tray and take two trays out at once. While one tray is being devoured, the other tray can be passed to the other side of the room.

Throwing a party without a hitch from start to finish is an art form. The list of steps to follow is long and, for some, intimidating. No worry, though, because with the aid of your notebook planner, determination, and thoroughness, you will glide through your event gracefully and graciously—all thanks to your smooth moves.

The Least You Need to Know

- Have someone act as cohost to alleviate any party problems.
- Clean as you cook to save time.
- Buffet serving solves space, time, and flow problems.
- Specialty food bars score well with guests.
- Set containers of snack foods all over the party place.

Part 4

Classic Occasions

There are a number of reasons why you might decide to throw a party. You might be looking to impress your new neighbors, the boss, or even your future in-laws. Whatever it might be, we've put together a part that will make it easy and painless for you.

There are just some classic occasions in life that every person must face, whether it's a cocktail party, a black-tie dinner, or a business dinner; you'll learn how to entertain these crowds with the greatest of ease. Not only will you impress them, but you'll impress yourself with what a fantastic host you really are.

Chapter 14

The Cocktail Hour

In This Chapter

- Serving food at your cocktail party
- Choosing wine for a wine-and-cheese party
- Planning a cocktail party for a large group
- Hiring a wine expert to help host your party

One of the most popular parties is the cocktail party. It usually starts between 4 and 7 P.M. and is relatively short—usually an hour or two—with a somewhat limited food selection. If you have never been to a cocktail party, think of it as happy hour at your favorite pub: a little food, a couple of drinks, a few laughs, and then back to your life.

It also can be a party that's held before another event. For instance, if you and friends are going out to dinner and a movie, you might get together for a couple of drinks first. It also might be the wrap-up after a get-together that's been too much fun to put an immediate end to. Whatever the reason, cocktail parties should be short and sweet.

If you are new to giving parties, hosting a cocktail event is a great way to put your big toe into the waters. And with the tips found in this chapter, you'll soon be a cocktail expert.

Party Pitfall

You will undoubtedly use more liquor and supplies if you make it a self-service bar. You may want to offset that by serving as bartender yourself or bringing in a professional.

Shindig Sayings

In years past, a **sommelier** was the steward or servant in charge of wines on large estates. These people were responsible for stocking, storing, and selecting wines for their employers.

Chips and Tips

Be prepared to have a clean glass for each guest for each wine. Paper or plastic are not good options as they affect the taste of the wine.

Belly Up to the Bar

Obviously, at a cocktail party you will want to serve drinks. It's not necessary that they be alcoholic, but those are the more traditional kind available to guests.

If you don't have an actual bar, you'll need to set up an area to serve as one. You will need two tables. The back bar is basically a work station. The front table is where the glass is placed for the guest to be served.

The best place to set up, if possible, is in the kitchen. It's easier to access ice, chilled glasses, and running water to wash glasses, pitchers, and shakers.

Best Cellars

Wine-and-cheese parties are probably the best known and most popular forms of cocktail parties.

If you're not familiar with wines, you can get a book on the subject, do some on-line research (www.epicurious.com is a great site), or check with the *sommelier* either at a liquor store that specializes in wine or your favorite fine restaurant. Be sure to let him know the price range of the wine you are interested in.

There are a lot of options in hosting a wine party. You can select a certain vineyard or producer (Perrier-Jouét, Berringer, Swanson Winery), type (Chablis, merlot, chardonnay), vintage (year), region (Bordeaux, Tuscany, Napa Valley), or a certain country. Some countries, like Australia, for one, are gaining a lot of popularity for its wines. Of course, France, Italy, Germany, and the United States are the most common.

You also will want to have a variety of cheeses to serve your guests. Remember, however, that you want the cheese to enhance, not detract from, the wine. Therefore, if you have chosen a variety of light wines, choose a light cheese.

The cheese is served with breads and crackers. Fruit—apples, pears, strawberries, peaches, and grapes are also delicious choices.

When planning your party, you will want at least four to six different wines and three to six different cheeses to accompany the wine.

Martini Madness

Another party that's taken on renewed popularity is a martini event. You will need to have a variety of vodkas (and possibly gins) to make a selection of these potent potables.

Proper glasses are a must for the martini mavens. Unless you are very up on what's popular, you might want to hire a bartender from a nearby martini bar or buy a book of martini recipes.

Festive Facts

W. C. Fields' propensity for drinking is legendary. Near the end of his life, he had severe liver trouble and bright red discoloration on his face due to excessive drinking. The studio makeup artists always had to apply heavy coats of cosmetics to hide his symptoms. Despite all that, the alcoholic funnyman was often seen drinking as much as 2 quarts of martinis a day.

Champagne and Caviar

For a truly special event, trot out the bubbly to wash down your caviar. Champagne is still the symbol of the ultimate celebration. So when it's time to wish the bridal couple well, celebrate an anniversary, praise a promotion, or just toast a milestone birthday, champagne is still the drink of choice.

In general, if you are going to serve champagne, it's best to go with a quality brand. Quality is easily discerned in champagne, even for someone who is not very experienced.

If you are serving champagne, the quality of your food should be appropriate to the occasion. That

Chips and Tips

When you are celebrating special occasions with champagne toasts, be sure to stock sparkling cider or other nonalcoholic bubbling beverages for those guests who prefer them.

means that you wouldn't want to spend a fortune on a bottle of wine to wash down a hamburger—unless that's your guest of honor's favorite food.

Try jazzing up your party with a little caviar. Caviar is traditionally served ice cold and on plain toast points. However, you might want to have these toppings available: finely chopped hard-boiled egg, minced onions, and sour cream.

Cutting the Cheese

Since you are not trying to feed people a meal at a cocktail party, the food served might be a variety of cheeses with crackers or a more elaborate spread of substantial appetizers. Remember, you always should serve food to help offset the liquor's effects.

For ease of serving, keep the food to one or two hot choices and one or two cold choices. Be sure these are small, bite-sized selections that require nothing more complicated than a fork to eat, and preferably just your hands or a toothpick.

Depending upon when you're hosting the party, the guidelines for appetizer quantities are as follows:

One-hour cocktail party before dinner:

3–4 light hors d'oeuvres per person

5–6 heavy hors d'oeuvres per person

One- to two-hour cocktail party without dinner:

5–8 light hors d'oeuvres per person

3–6 heavy hors d'oeuvres per person

5–8 combination of hot and cold per person

Great food, exceptional drinks, and pleasurable socializing are the makings of an event that is guaranteed to put you in the Hosts' Hall of Fame.

Chips and Tips

For a novel way to present bite-size appetizers, stick plastic forks or fancy toothpicks, holding the snack, into a melon half with the flat side down of the fruit on the dish. The picks will give a porcupine look to the melon.

Chips and Tips

Be sure to cover easily damaged surfaces like wood, marble, and glass with felt-back plastic tablecloths. You can cover these with lovely fabric to preserve your decor and party theme.

Beating the Balancing Act

Even though the typical cocktail party atmosphere is one of mixing and mingling, some seating is necessary.

You can make eating-while-standing more manageable for your guests if you clear off the tops of furniture to make room for guests to park their drinks, or rent bar-height tables. Provide napkins or coasters, to absorb the moisture on glasses.

Since the cocktail party is quite uncomplicated and takes less time to plan than a full-blown party, it can be produced on short notice to acknowledge or celebrate any occasion in a spontaneous way. Just by keeping a bare minimum of party essentials on hand, you can throw together frequent and fast festivities that may rival those that have been planned for weeks.

The Least You Need to Know

- A cocktail party can take place before or after dinner.
- When planning a wine-and-cheese party, make sure the two compliment each other.
- Open-house cocktail parties are ideal for large groups.
- Frequent and spontaneous celebrations are easy with cocktail parties.

Chapter 15

Black-Tie Affair

In This Chapter

- Setting a formal table
- Knowing which fork to use and when to use it
- Planning a multicourse meal
- Serving your guests

While most parties you play host to will be more along the lines of simple, one- or two-course meals, buffets, chips and dip, or pizza-and-beer gatherings, there will be times when you will need to entertain a little more formally.

Since most of us haven't been to finishing school and don't practice strict dining etiquette in our day-to-day lives, this chapter will teach you (or refresh) some skills you will need to be the perfect host no matter the situation. This way, when it comes time for you to pop the question, impress your boss, or meet your future in-laws, you will have the tools to entertain with confidence and panache.

Turning the Table

If you plan to entertain formally, it's important that you understand that this meal cannot be served on snack trays or on the kitchen counter. Ideally, a formal meal is served in a formal dining room. However, if you don't have a traditional dining set, you still can make accommodations for an elegant event. Dining tables and chairs can easily be rented for under $15.

Party Pitfall

Test the height of any extra chairs you put at the table. You'd hate for some people to be sitting so low that their chins are resting on their plates, or other guests so high they have to bend over just to see under the light fixture.

Chips and Tips

Choosing the right guest list is one of the most important ingredients to a good dinner party. You want the conversation lively, not combative or uncomfortable. Select guests who have similar interests and temperaments and blend well together.

It's not a good idea to cramp your guests. When you are seated at a dining table for the bulk of the evening, tight seating isn't cozy, it's annoying. Either rethink your guest list, or put together two dining tables.

Limiting the Guest List

Wherever you decide to hold the dinner party, try to invite no more guests than you have seats at one table. However, when a large guest list can't be avoided, you need to set up a second table. Do this only if you can keep the tables close to each other so guests sitting at the second table don't feel as if they have been invited to a different party.

If you are forced to have two separate tables, make certain that each table is decorated comparably. Also, be sure to place one host (if necessary, appoint a co-host) at each table so guests won't think they have been placed at "the kid's table."

Counting Courses

A formal meal may have anywhere from three courses on up. There are even some gastronomical journeys that have dozens of courses. While that might sound appealing to a guest, it probably seems frightening to a host. Chances are you will probably have only five courses to your meal. Trust us, this isn't as bad as it sounds. You will likely start the meal with an appetizer (possibly even served during a cocktail hour), then move on to a fish dish (oysters, clams, mussels, or shrimp cocktail), then a soup and/or salad. Then you will proceed into the entreé, and follow that with dessert.

There is remarkable flexibility in designing the menu for your formal dinner. However, take into consideration your guests' tastes and ease of preparation. Don't prepare a menu that will keep you in the kitchen longer than you will be in the dining room.

Creating the Cuisine

What you choose to serve is even more varied than the amount and types of courses acceptable.

Etiquette dictates it is important you have the proper dining service to present each course properly. In other words, if you don't have a special fish fork, you shouldn't serve a fish course to start your meal.

Now, let's get practical. Most people don't know what a fish fork looks like, much less own one; it seems silly that you would reject your best fish recipe just because you don't own the right fork. However, if at all possible, at least provide a clean knife, fork, and/or spoon with each course as needed.

Chips and Tips

Do keep in mind that if you choose to offer multiple courses, keep the portions small so guests won't fill up before they reach the main course.

When Money's No Object

If you can afford to choose whatever meal you wish to serve, feel free to create a menu with multiple courses and an extensive wine list. While this type of meal is generally reserved for a gourmet cook and friends who appreciate fine dining, it is fun to do on occasion.

Chips and Tips

No matter how much or how little you will be spending on your meal, ask your guests if they have any dietary restrictions. Or simply make certain you have extra vegetables available should someone arrive and announce they are allergic to fish, don't eat meat, or are on some particular diet.

Chef's Choice

Create menus with any dishes you feel comfortable cooking. Don't forget there are many excellent package mixes to help you as well. There is no rule that says you must cook everything from scratch. Consommé, for instance, can be made by heating canned beef broth and adding a splash of sherry. You don't have to create the dish by making beef stock from bones.

Tempting Takeout

Let's assume you've inherited a full set of china, crystal, and silverware, but unfortunately you didn't inherit any cooking skills. Can you still serve a formal meal? Of course. Remember that presentation is the key, so grab your takeout menus or head to your favorite gourmet delicatessen.

When hosting a dinner party, it is usually not your cooking skills that are being judged but your ability as a host. Don't let your lack of cooking skills prevent you from hosting an elegant event.

Festive Facts

A society woman was a great cook, loved to entertain, and enjoyed giving formal dinner parties. One day she inadvertently ruined a batch of chicken piccata just before her guests were scheduled to arrive. She placed a call to a local Italian restaurant, which surreptitiously delivered enough to serve her guests, and kept it warm in her oven. When it came time to serve the entreé, she replated the meal onto her china dinner plates.

As dinner proceeded, one of her guests remarked that the meat tasted remarkably like that served at the restaurant. The hostess simply said, "Yes, it's the same recipe. I hope you're enjoying it." That's grace under pressure!

Eliminate Experiments

One of the most common mistakes beginning hosts make is trying a recipe for the first time on their guests. Even experienced chefs can only guess what a recipe might taste like from studying the ingredients.

Chips and Tips

When you serve multiple courses with multiple selections of wine, you start with a mild course and mild wine, working your way up to heavier tastes in both food and wine as the courses progress.

If a recipe sounds appealing, try it out first on your family or a close friend or two. Don't let it be the possible ruination of your dinner party.

Perfect Place Settings

You may have purchased or been given a standard set of china. This generally consists of eight to twelve place settings, each with a dinner plate, bread/salad/dessert plate, soup bowl, cup, and saucer.

A typical flatware place setting consists of a dinner fork, salad/dessert fork, teaspoon, table/soup spoon, and a butter knife with a serrated edge. Add other pieces as your budget or needs dictate.

Formal glasses do not generally come in sets and are purchased by the piece or type. However, you should have a stemmed water glass and a wine glass at the minimum for each guest. (A complete list of bar glasses is included in Chapter 9, "Tiny Bubbles: Stocking Your Bar").

Topping the Tablescape

As host, it is up to you (or your waitstaff) to set the table. It is therefore important that you understand how place settings are laid out.

Since you know the menu, make sure there are a sufficient number of dishes, glasses, and flatware for each course. At the beginning of the meal, it is not necessary to have any more plates on the table than is required for the first course and bread plates.

Chips and Tips

If you own service for eight and you have ten or twelve guests, rent or borrow half as many place settings as you will need in total plus one. This will enable you to alternate the dishes at every seat and have one left over just in case.

Setting Up

The dinner or first-course plate is centered to each chair and placed one inch from the edge of the table. The bread-and-butter plate is placed at 11 o'clock to the dinner plate. The knife is placed horizontally and at the top of the bread plate with the handle pointing to the right.

Keep in mind, no round bowl should be presented without a flat plate under it. This means if you were to offer salad or soup in a bowl, you would not put it on the table without a flat plate underneath it.

You may preset the dinner plate under the first-course plate, but it is not necessary. However, if you do, you might wish to place a doily on top of the dinner plate so it will remain clean should something accidentally get spilled from the first course. The doily would be removed when the first-course dishes are taken away.

Chips and Tips

To help you remember whether a piece of flatware goes to the left or right of a plate, remember the word *left* has four letters, and so does *fork*. *Knife* and *spoon* each contain five letters and so does the word *right*.

Use Your Utensils

Forks (except fish forks) are always placed to the left of the plate; knives and spoons go to the right.

Depending upon what would be needed for your meal, the forks would be laid out to the left of the plate. The largest piece is centered on the dish, and all the other pieces are lined up so the bottoms of the pieces form a straight line. Lay them out according to the menu items served and going from left to right: cocktail fork, salad fork, and dinner fork. On the other side of the plate, you would line up the knives and spoon. Starting from the inside and moving right there are: steak knife, dinner knife, fish knife or fish fork, and soup spoon.

Chips and Tips

If you have a proper fish fork with a heavy left tine, that can be used to replace the fish knife.

Generally the soup spoon is the only spoon preset. However, you might place a dessert spoon above the dinner plate and horizontal to it with the bowl facing left.

If you were to also preset the dessert fork, it would be placed below the dessert spoon and facing the opposite direction.

A teaspoon, if needed, is placed on the saucer with the cup when dessert is served.

Properly set flatware.

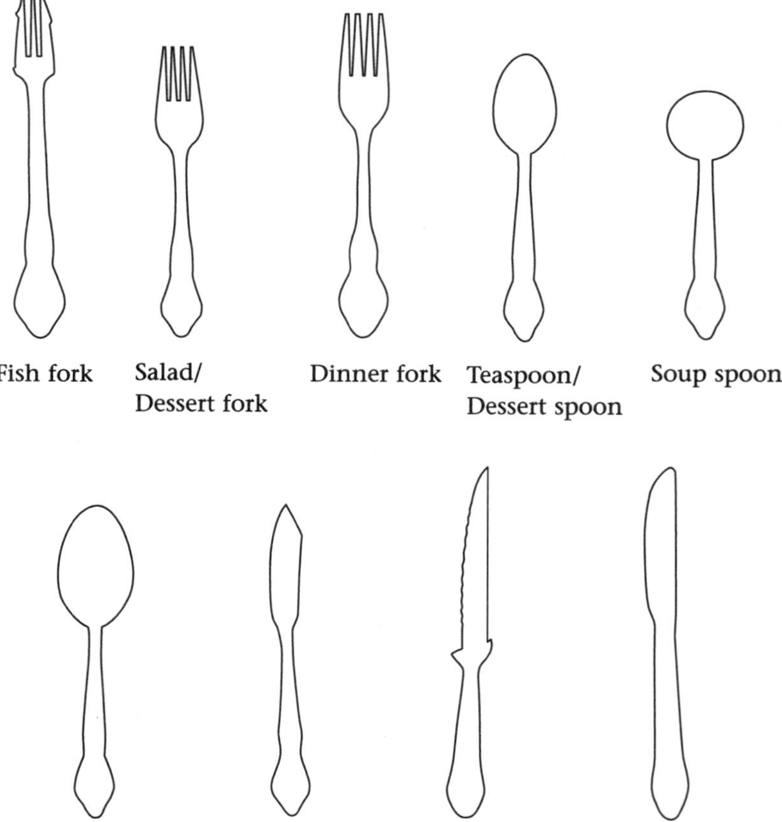

Wash It Down

The glasses start with the water glass set at the 1 o'clock position to your plate and one to two inches away. The red-wine glass goes below and to the right, the white-wine glass goes below and to the right of that, and the champagne flute just below and to the right of the white-wine glass.

Wiping Up

The napkin can be placed to the left of the first fork, folded and placed inside an empty glass, or placed on top of your dishes if you are not presetting any of the courses. If you are serving a formal dinner you might want to consider renting, borrowing, or even buying cloth napkins.

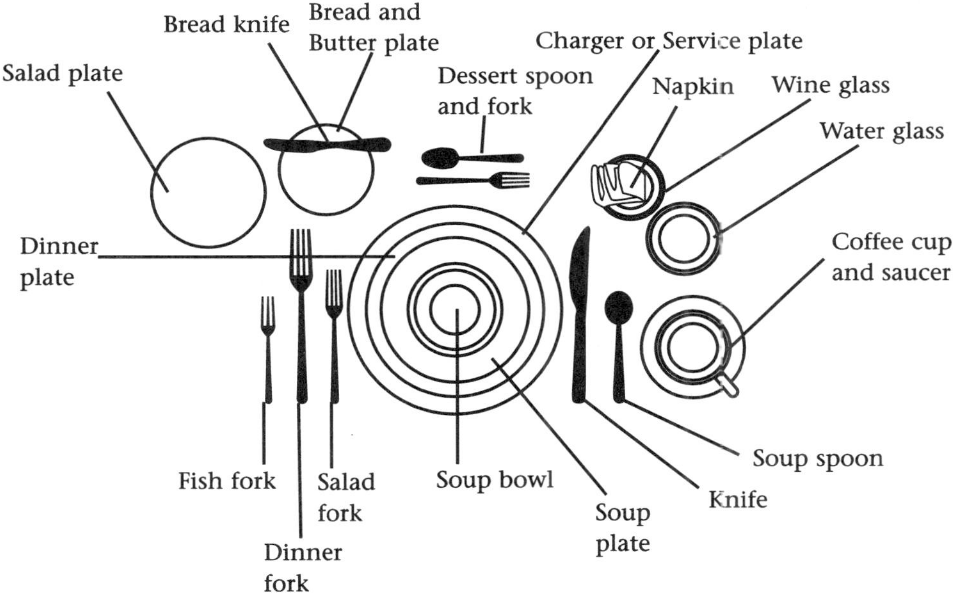

A formal place setting.

Charge It

For a very elegant presentation, you should use a *charger* or *service plate*. These are large, round platters that are put at each place setting under the dinner plate. Food is never served on the charger. It may be removed when the first course is served or the first course's plate may be placed on the charger.

Finishing Touches

As you would expect, there is more to a formal table than plates, flatware, and glasses. Here are a few things you should consider when putting together your tablescape.

Shindig Sayings

A **charger** or **service plate** is a large round platter that is put under or instead of a dinner plate as decoration only.

Where Do I Sit?

While you can leave open seating at your dining table, it is far better to assign places.

These can be made from heavy paper stock folded in half with the guest's name beautifully inscribed or printed on your computer's printer. You could also put the paper in a small picture frame, which becomes a momento to take home. There is almost a limitless variety of ways to let your guests know where to sit.

Chips and Tips

Take an instant photo of your guests upon arrival, or use a picture from past occasions and frame the picture as the place setting and memento.

When planning a seating chart, it is very important to consider your guests when setting the seats:

- Do not put a left-handed guest in the middle of a table of right-handers
- Place elderly guests or those in wheelchairs closest to the restroom or at the ends of the table
- Seat yourself so you can easily get up to refresh drinks and serve guests
- Separate couples to promote a lively conversation
- Only put in a male/female seating pattern if there is an even number of guests
- Place a shy guest next to a gregarious one who will draw that person out

Center of Attention

A centerpiece is usually used to bring color and style to your dining table. It is often made of flowers, but you can use a variety of items to suit a particular theme if you are having one.

The most important thing to remember about a centerpiece is that it should be below eye level or raised on a transparent platform above eye level to avoid interfering with your guests' line of vision and conversation.

Serving with Style

While you may preset your first course, you will need to determine how you are going to serve the rest of the meal. You must choose whether you are going to give your guests plated portions or have the guests served by you or a waitstaff member. Do not place the food in serving dishes and leave it on the table for guests to help themselves at a formal dinner.

Chips and Tips

If you are unsure whether a centerpiece is too high, place your elbow next to the arrangement and raise your arm straight up. If the centerpiece is above your middle finger, it is too high.

Plated Portions

This is the most practical serving solution. It allows you to portion out the servings in your kitchen uniformly. This is important if you plan to serve multiple courses and want to serve small allotments of each dish. It also allows you to arrange the food on the dish attractively. Sprinkle herbs or colorful spices around the edge of the plate to give it color and to make the plate seem more full.

Chips and Tips

If there is only one portion, it should be centered on the plate. When there are several foods, each should be given a distinct section of the plate.

Serve from the Left

Whether you choose to bring each dish around for the guests to serve themselves, or the food will be served by you or a waitstaff member, serve from the left.

The logic behind this custom is that the majority of people are right-handed. This would allow them to use their right hand if they are serving themselves.

Likewise, when the diners have finished their course, you should remove the plate from the right.

Keep in mind that there should always be a plate in front of your guest and that glasses are not removed until dessert is served.

Hiring Help

Should you decide you would like to hire someone to help serve the meal, there are a number of places to check.

If there is a culinary institute or hospitality management program at your local college, these students are usually trained in the art of presentation. However, be sure it is a student who has almost completed the program, not a beginner.

You also might check at your favorite fine restaurant (not the pizza parlor) for a lead. If your regular waiter is not available, he might be able to suggest someone else.

Party Pitfall

Unless you are thoroughly experienced yourself, do not attempt to train someone to serve guests. Despite popular belief, formal serving is a practiced art.

Do make sure you tell the waitstaff member how you would prefer he or she dresses. All of them are capable of supplying their own uniform to a degree (slacks, white shirt, and tie). However, fancy vests, dinner jackets, or evening coats might have to be provided if you require these. Many waitresses will own the equivalent costuming, but might not have a formal maid's uniform.

Whether you are serving the meal yourself or hiring someone to do it for you, the most important thing to remember is to relax, enjoy yourself, and sit back and wait for the compliments on what an excellent hostess you are.

The Least You Need to Know

- ➤ Formal dining refers primarily to the presentation.
- ➤ Place flatware from out to in, in the order it will be used.
- ➤ Forks go to the left, spoons and knives to the right.
- ➤ If hiring a waitstaff person, make sure they have appropriate experience or training.